Knowledge, Education and Learning

– E-learning in the Knowledge Society

LARS QVORTRUP

Samfundslitteratur Press

Lars Qvortrup
Knowledge, Education and Learning – E-learning in the Knowledge Society
1. edition 2006

© Samfundslitteratur Press, 2006

Cover: Imperiet
Typeset: Samfundslitteratur
Print: Narayana Press, Gylling, Denmark

ISBN-10: 87-593-1249-1
ISBN-13: 978-87-593-1249-0

Published by:
Samfundslitteratur Press
Rosenoerns Allé 9
DK-1970 Frederiksberg C
Tel.: +45 38 15 38 80
forlagetsl@sl.cbs.dk
www.forlagetsl.dk

ation

ning

ng in the
e Society

Content

Series Introduction

Present-day society is often referred to as a *knowledge society*.

But how can knowledge be defined and what role does it play, along with the related or connected concepts of learning and media/ICT? In what sense does learning lead to knowledge, what forms of learning are adequate in the so-called knowledge society, and how are appropriate forms of learning underpinned? How should media be conceptualised, and what is the role of the media, not least digital media, i.e. ICT, in society?

These are the basic questions to which the series "Knowledge, Learning and Media/ICT" is devoted.

Series editor: Lars Qvortrup, professor of media research at University of Southern Denmark, Odense, director of Knowledge Lab DK.

Introduction

Most people seem to agree that we live in a "Knowledge Society" and that a basic current challenge is to accelerate the so-called "Knowledge Economy".

But what is "knowledge", which seems to have become a basic political and sociological category? For good reasons, policy makers don't bother to find out. It is not their business to analyse society, but to make policy. However, the same seems to be the case in the sociological literature. If you go through the literature, no satisfactory answer can be found. Sometimes, it is simply admitted and accepted that the concept is slippery. At other times, although suggestions for definitions can be found, they are both mutually incompatible and – with a few exceptions – inherently logically unclear.

Similarly, most people agree that in order to put the "knowledge society" into reality, learning – even life-long learning – is a necessary precondition. Therefore, "learning" is another favourite concept, and the "learning society" another frequently used term.

But again, nobody really seems to know, how "learning" should be defined or put into reality. One can see that others learn, but it is hard to explain why they do so. What is the distinction between learning and socialisation (can all personal change be defined as learning?), and what is the distinction and relationship between learning and teaching? Is it, in the literal sense, possible to "make" people learn, and is this done through teaching? What is it actual role of the educational system, and does it expand – or does it gradually disappear – in a so-called "Learning Society" in which everybody is supposed to learn perpetually and everywhere?

What skills should be achieved? Should we aim at increasing the basic qualifications defined as factual knowledge, or should we rather go for competencies, i.e. for practical skills concerned with problem solving etc.? Here, answers differ. While politicians often seem to be in favour of easily measurable factual knowledge, industrialists and employers seem to prefer problem-solving competencies, abilities to work in teams, innovation skills etc. At least, this part of the debate points to the fact that knowledge is many things, and that we need a vocabulary in order to compare different forms of knowledge and skills.

And finally: How do we speed up knowledge development and learning? The standard answer is: Through technologies. The argument seems to be that as industrial production is more efficient than pre-industrial production, so should e-learning (or e-teaching) be better than plain, unplugged learning. But is this really so? Can learning and teaching be speeded up and can its productivity be raised by introducing digital tools and technologies?

The present book is small, yet ambitious. It aims at answering all these basic questions.

In the first chapter a definition and categorisation of knowledge is presented. Knowledge is defined as confirmed observations, and it is suggested that the general effect of knowledge is the ability to manage complexity, because the effect of knowledge is to provide a horizon of expectations. Something is observed and then observed again – by myself or by others – and through this process the surprise of the initial observation ("look what happens when you enter an automatic door") is transformed into expectations, i.e. into knowledge (about doors and other phenomena). As a matter of fact, the basic function of the educational system is to collect knowledge and provide others with knowledge in form of condensed observations. Normally the knowledge of the educational system is produced by another functional system, which has specialised in deciding when observations have been condensed and confirmed in such a way that they can be called scientific knowledge: the research system. Thus, the educational system is operationally coupled to the scientific system, e.g. through textbooks that translate scientific knowledge into didactically mediated knowledge.

Based on this definition, knowledge can be structured into a logical system of knowledge categories: Factual knowledge, competence, creative knowledge and culture. When I say that this system is logical, the principle is the following: Factual knowledge is knowledge of objects and phenomena. It is first order knowledge. Competence is knowledge about factual knowledge, e.g. knowledge about how to solve problems by using one's factual knowledge. This is thus second order knowledge: Knowledge of knowledge. Creative knowledge is knowledge about knowledge about knowledge, i.e. knowledge about the hidden assumptions and/or explicated theories on which problem solving is practised. It is called "creative" because the possession of this type of knowledge makes it possible to change or modify one's basic and often implicit assumptions and thus to do or "know" something differently. This, then, is third order knowledge. Finally, fourth order knowledge is knowledge concerning the evolutionary background for our system of knowledge forms. This fourth order knowledge cannot be changed or modified by the individual knowing person, but we know that it exists as the cultural knowledge background, i.e. as that which constitutes the absolute borderline to that which cannot be known. We know that we don't know what we don't know.

In the second chapter learning and teaching are defined and categorised in a similar system. There is not one way of learning, but indeed many. However, referring to the categories of knowledge four different learning levels can be identified, from simple learning defined as accumulation of facts, through assimilative and accommodative learning into learning as an evolutionary process of collective change. Similarly, there is not just one way of teaching, but different teaching categories can be identified depending on which type of learning is to be stimulated.

The third chapter is about media pedagogy. What is pedagogy? According to the definition suggested in this book, didactics is reflection of teaching, cf. the well-known theory of the reflective practitioner. Thus, didactics is teaching methods. Compared with didactics, pedagogy is second order teaching reflection. It is reflection of didactics, i.e. speculations concerning the basis of teaching methods or reflections about the way in which the reflective practitioner reflects.

In practical terms, one could say that in the classroom the reflective teacher does didactics, while in the staff room together with his or her colleagues the teacher practises pedagogy. They reflect their teaching methods.

Thus, media pedagogy is second order reflection of the relationship between teaching and media. This relationship is threefold: It concerns media education, i.e. teaching about media and how to use media. It concerns media socialisation, i.e. teaching of pupils who live in and are socialised by a media society. And it concerns educational media, i.e. the use of media – and particularly: digital media – in and for teaching.

This then leads into the fourth chapter about e-learning. "E-learning" is the standard European word for the use of digital media or technologies in and for teaching. During the past 30 years, great things have been expected of e-learning. New, digital media should remove the "barriers" of learning, it was assumed, as if learning was the result of transportation of information or knowledge from the teacher to the student, or from one – knowledge-intensive – region to a knowledge-poor region.

Evaluation results and ordinary experience have demonstrated that this isn't the way in which teaching and learning work. Teaching is not transportation of knowledge, and learning is not reception of knowledge from an outside "sender" or "provider" of information. This type of critique then led to the opposite idea: that e-learning isn't at all possible. One can only learn face-to-face with the master, was the reaction. However, this antithetical position isn't fair: Can't you learn by reading books or by doing things on your own? Of course you can – and if you couldn't, you should immediately stop reading the present book. The problem thus is not to choose sides in the either-or distinction. The problem is the distinction itself. The precondition for understanding the function of analogue and digital media in education is to realise that teaching and learning are two different and mutually separated phenomena: Teaching is communication, for instance in the interaction system constituted by the classroom, while learning is a cognitive process in meaning-based systems. Consequently, what media – including digital media – can provide is structural couplings between classroom communication and learning.

The chapter summarises four theories of e-learning in order to demonstrate that each theory provides special expectations to teaching, learning and the effect and use of e-learning. The chapter concludes by suggesting that e-learning can be categorised according to the same four categories of knowledge that have been used in the preceding chapters.

The final chapter presents the theoretical source of inspiration for the book: The German sociologist Niklas Luhmann's theory of knowledge, learning, teaching and education, which he elaborated and constantly developed and modified in a large number of articles and books – many of which he edited together with Karl Eberhard Schorr. All these findings were summarised in his last book, the one about society's educational system: *Das Erziehungssystem der Gesellschaft,* which was published posthumously by Dieter Lenzen in 2002. It is, however, important to emphasize that Luhmann has not presented us with a ready-to-use set of knowledge categories. The system of knowledge categories is totally my own responsibility. I have, however, been immensely stimulated and inspired by Luhmann's sociological theory. It turns the well-known world upside down. It is a contra-intuitive theoretical machinery. Everybody should be rewarded with the opportunity to challenge his or her standard beliefs by reading just a bit – one or two books – of Luhmann's oeuvre.

When I wrote this book I tried to make everything as clear and simple as possible. However, behind this small book lie several years of hard work. The content is based on three books in Danish: *Det hyperkomplekse samfund* (The Hypercomplex Society) from 1998, *Det lærende samfund* (The Learning Society) from 2001, and *Det vidende samfund* (The Knowing Society) from 2004. Parts of the first two books were used as inputs for the American book *The Hypercomplex Society* from 2003, which is thus not a translation of the Danish book with the same title.

Based on these books and the present small "milestone" I have launched a new ambitious personal project: One book on each of the four categories of knowledge. I am currently working on the book about the fourth category of knowledge, that which constitutes the horizon of possible knowledge, i.e. of knowing that we cannot know what we cannot know, or of knowing that the more we know, the more we know that we don't know. This form of knowledge constitutes the knowledge about the borders between knowledge and non-knowledge.

The history of the knowledge of non-knowledge is rich. According to my studies, in Europe it started with Saint Augustine's fifteen books *De trinitate* from 399-419 AD. But this is another story, which will be presented in another book.

Acknowledgment

Thanks to my colleagues at Knowledge Lab DK and at the research programme Knowledge, Learning and Media/ICT for ideas and feedback. Thanks to John Irons for providing linguistic support.

1. Knowledge Society, Knowledge and Knowledge Categories

Introduction

We are in a paradoxical situation.

On the one hand almost everybody seems to agree that knowledge is a basic phenomenon of and an adequate basic concept for our current society. Very few would dispute that we live in a "knowledge society", that it is important to develop "knowledge intensive" enterprises, or that the knowledge production of research and educational institutions is central for the reproduction of the wealth of our nations.

On the other hand, we do not seem to know how knowledge should be defined within the context of a theory of society. Most of the current theories of knowledge society, knowledge production and knowledge intensive enterprises do not suggest an explicit concept of knowledge, and even if they do, the concept is a narrow one – so narrow that it does not inform the knowledge production practice of educational institutions.

In this chapter I will first demonstrate that the above, critical statement concerning current knowledge society theories is relevant and true. Secondly, I will present an elaborated concept of knowledge, a concept that can be used for developing a theory of forms of knowledge that can inform the understanding of the functional mechanisms of the so-called knowledge society and the design and contribution of educational practices.

According to my theory of knowledge, knowledge can be categorised into four forms: 1st, 2nd, 3rd and 4th order knowledge. After having presented and exemplified the concept and the categories of knowledge, in chapter two I will demonstrate the relevance of the knowledge categories in the context of education. Corresponding to the four categories of knowledge, four forms of teaching and learning can be identified. Similarly, the way in which learning should be evaluated of course depends on the type of knowledge in question. Finally, I will demonstrate that the knowledge categories can inform the identification of strategies for the teacher's self-reflection and thus can qualify the teacher as a reflective practitioner.

The ultimate aim is to develop a theoretical basis for educating the professional teacher, assuming that the days have past when teaching was an activity based only on common sense. In a knowledge society teaching is a professional activity founded in research based evidence (cf. OECD 2005).

Current Knowledge Theories

It seems to be generally agreed upon that present-day society is rapidly moving away from observing itself as an industrial society, the basic function of which was to develop mechanical systems of production and organisation that could transform nature into industrial products, towards a knowledge society, the basic function of which is to handle complexity with the aid of knowledge, no matter whether this knowledge exists as a resource in the individual worker or as knowledge systems in companies and organisations.

150 years ago, Karl Marx confronted a similar challenge: the capitalist society developing into its industrial phase. His answer to this challenge and to his aim of understanding the functional mechanisms of capitalism was to identify and to analyse the basic "atom" of that society: The commodity.

The fundamental challenge of creating a theory of society is to choose an adequate starting point, or – in a post-ontological jargon – to make an adequate, initial distinction. For Karl Marx this starting point was: the commodity. For him this was the atom of capitalist society. Based on a post-metaphysical understanding and thus replacing identity – "atoms" – with differences – "distinctions" – we would call it the marked state of the initial distinction (cf. Spencer Brown 1971 and Clam 2002 and 2004). Anyway, Marx created what became a normative distinction between a commoditised society versus a (utopian) non-commoditised society. In the second half of the 20th Century Jürgen Habermas suggested another basic distinction: For him the marked state of the initial distinction was named life world – assuming that the unmarked state is systems: A non-mediated life world based on free individuals aiming at consensus versus the systems mediated by symbolically generalised media aiming at efficiency. At the same time, the German sociologist Niklas Luhmann suggested yet another initial distinction, namely: system versus environment.

Of course, scientific concepts form the contact of science with reality (cf. Luhmann 1995 p. li). Therefore, selecting an initial distinction is to decide upon a particular contact with reality, and not others. The question is whether this contact is more adequate than others. Still, however, the basic problem of making an initial distinction is that "...[e]very conceptual determination ought to be read as a constraint on the possibility of further conceptual determination." (Ibid. p. l). With the choice of an initial distinction the sociological observer of society starts the building of a conceptual system that cannot lead anywhere, but – if the concepts are solid – is self-restricting.

Thus, Marx chose "the commodity" as his starting point and developed a theory of production and circulation of commodities and capital as a self-limiting context for the observation of society. In *Soziale Systeme* Luhmann chose "system" as *his* initial distinction. He decided that "systems" defined through the concept of autopoiesis should be the starting point for developing his self-restricting system of concepts. Marx developed one set of restrictions for the observation of society, Luhmann developed another set. For both, the consequence was that some parts of reality could be better observed than others. Developing a theoretical paradigm, some phenomena will be enlightened while others will be less clearly seen.

Similarly, in order to observe society as a knowledge society and to understand the functional mechanisms of an emerging knowledge society – or, as I would prefer: a knowing society – one should focus on the marked state of this society: knowledge, and thus implying that knowledge/non-knowledge is an adequate basic distinction.

But in order to test whether this initial distinction is adequate, the concept must be taken seriously. It must be defined in such a way that it is robust as the basis for further conceptual determinations. What is knowledge? Which knowledge categories can be identified?

In most theories of the knowledge society, any explicit, sociologically relevant definition of knowledge is absent. As early as 1959, the

English economist and organisation analyst Edith Penrose emphasised the growing importance of knowledge in economy, but in addition she admitted that the whole subject of knowledge is so "slippery" that it is impossible to get a firm grip of it (Penrose 1959 p. 77). In 1969 Peter Drucker announced that knowledge has become the central capital, cost centre and basic resource of the economy (Drucker 1969 p. ix). Still however he did not suggest how to appropriately define this basic resource. Approximately thirty years later, Luhmann correctly summarised: "...was is Wissen? Wenn man von der Gesellschaftstheorie ausgeht und selbst wenn man die moderne Gesellschaft als 'Wissensgesellschaft' bezeichnet, findet man keinen brauchbaren Begriff des Wissens." (Luhmann 2002 p. 97)

However, in some of the theories subscribing to the knowledge society idea, definitions of knowledge have been suggested. Still, to my mind these definitions are not adequate.

Sometimes, often in relation to information and communication technologies (ICTs), knowledge is defined as an essence or substance, cf. for instance the OECD report from 2004, *Innovation in the Knowledge Economy*, which focuses on "implications for education and learning". Here, it is emphasised that it is important to have a clear idea of "...what it is that is passing through the electronic pipelines: knowledge, information or data?" (OECD 2004 p. 18). However, the challenges of education and learning – why doesn't teaching automatically lead to adequate learning, if teaching is only a matter of transporting knowledge? – and of knowledge sharing – why is knowledge sharing actually most often *not* happening automatically? – cannot be answered if it is assumed that knowledge is a substance that can easily be transported from one person to the other. It is well known that this is *not* what happens in the classroom or in the knowledge-sharing organisation. Knowledge about something is a representation of something according to interpretation standards, which may change from person to person and from teacher to pupil. My knowledge is not equal to your knowledge, and it cannot be "transported" from me to you.

Also, ICT should not be subsumed under the general concept of technology as a tool for physical manipulation. As Joseph Weizenbaum demonstrated many years ago, ICT does not belong to the class of prosthetic technologies, but to the class of non-prosthetic technologies (Weizenbaum 1976). ICT should not be compared to hammers or spades or cars, with which you perform a physical manipulation or transportation of physical stuff. No, ICT is much closer related to sign technologies like books, images, posters or watches. A watch does not move time, it *represents* time. Similarly, ICT does not function as a physical transportation or manipulation machine, but as a sign medium and sign processor.

In other contexts, knowledge has been defined in a restricted way as certified knowledge. In his classical book about the post-industrial society Daniel Bell defined knowledge as "...a set of organised statements of facts or ideas, presenting a reasoned judgment or an experimental result, which is transmitted to others through some communication medium is some systematic form" (Bell 1973 p. 175). In his book about the network society, Manuel Castells has, as he says, "no compelling reason to improve on" this definition (Castells 1996 p. 17). But certified knowledge is only one aspect of knowledge, as for instance Michael Polanyi has convincingly argued. Also, tacit knowledge – the knowledge of e.g. how to ride a bike – is knowledge, although it cannot be written down or "proved" and certified in any traditionally scientific way.

In the 2004 OECD report this is reflected upon by making a distinction between on the one hand certified (tested) and practical (uncertified) knowledge, or in French: between "savoir" and "connaissance", and on the other hand between codified and tacit knowledge (OECD 2004 p. 18ff), and although no systematic categorisation of knowledge forms is provided, at least it is made clear that the question of knowledge is complex.

Yet another systematisation has been suggested by Bengt-Aake Lundvall in the OECD 2000 report *Knowledge Management in the Learning Society.* Here he suggests a categorisation into four forms of knowledge:

- Know-what that refers to knowledge about facts;
- know-why that refers to knowledge about principles and laws governing facts
- know-how that refers to skills, i.e. abilities to do something with one's factual knowledge;
- know-who that refers to the ability to trace knowledge providers across disciplines and specialisations (OECD 2000 p. 14f).

While I agree to some of these categories, I think the fourth knowledge form, "know-who" falls outside the paradigm hidden behind the categories.

A different theory of knowledge and knowledge categories has been developed by Max H. Boisot (1995 and 1998). In a way that can be compared with the one that I am proposing in the next section, Boisot conceptualizes knowledge as "...a set of probability distributions held by an agent and orienting his or her actions." (Boisot 1998 p. 12). Boisot suggests a typology of knowledge depending on whether it is diffused/undiffused and codified/uncodified. This leads into four categories of knowledge: Personal knowledge (undiffused and uncodified), common-sense knowledge (diffused and uncodified), proprietary knowledge (undiffused and codified), and public knowledge (diffused and codified) (Boisot 1995 p. 145-149). Based on these categories and adding a third dimension, i.e. abstraction, Boisot has suggested a description of the use and distribution of knowledge in organisations within the so-called Information-Space or just I-Space. In particular, a social learning cycle can be identified as a movement of knowledge – or information – within the I-Space (cf. Boisot 1995 p. 184ff). While this theory provides an understanding of the contextual effects on knowledge, it does not provide a logical theory of knowledge categories based on inherent qualities of knowledge.

My conclusion on this brief review of existing sociological knowledge theories is that we must leave the model of knowledge as an essence, which can be transported from place from place, i.e. from the research laboratory to the enterprise. Similarly, we must give up the idea that knowledge as suggested by Bell and Castells can be defined only as certified knowledge. For me, the concept of knowledge is multidimensional, and it cannot be perceived as something, which is created and certified in the ivory tower of research and then – sometimes via the educational sector – transferred to society in general and to the business sector in particular.

The Mystery of Knowledge

The Weird World of "Mind vs. Reality"

I hope that it is by now obvious that there is a job to do in order to unveil the mysteries of knowledge in the context of the knowledge society, and that this job is both important and demanding.

One of the problems of understanding knowledge and of developing a sociologically adequate concept of knowledge is that there is a mismatch between the understanding of society and the understanding of knowledge. While society is described in its current form as "post-industrial", "post-modern" etc., assuming that realities have changed during the latest hundred years, knowledge is still understood through classical epistemologies. The problem is a problem concerning theoretical a-synchronicity. I will briefly demonstrate, that the understanding of knowledge is based on an epistemology developed by Descartes and classical philosophy, while the understanding of society is post-Cartesian: It is – although most often implicitly – based on 20th century sociological theories informed by Husserl, Heidegger and others.

According to Cartesian philosophy, the world can be divided into *res cogitans* and *res extensa*. The thinking subject versus the external – not-thinking – world. Consequently, knowledge is the result of a correspondence between mind and world.

Thus, to know something is to establish a link or a correspondence between mind and reality. Just listen to the words: A "link". "Mind versus reality " – as if mind isn't reality, and as if thoughts are models "corresponding" to an external world. According to this world-view, to know something is to transport knowledge from the external world into the mind. Consequently, knowledge is the store of facts (in the computer age: the memory of information), and to share knowledge is to transfer knowledge from one file to another.

Still, most epistemological theory implicitly assumes that this weird world of correspondences, of minds outside reality and realities outside mind, constitutes the indisputable precondition for talking about knowledge. You may disagree about what comes first. You may be "realist" or "antirealist". Still, however, the very distinction between mind and reality is beyond discussion (for a recent example see Klausen 2004).

In accordance with this theory, modern knowledge management theory defines knowledge as a substance. Knowledge management is equal to management of physical processes. It is a theory about how to file, to transport and to provide access to knowledge substances.

Critique of "the ghost in the machine" paradigm

Inspired by e.g. Edmund Husserl's critique of the Cartesian philosophy, in 1949 the English language philosopher Gilbert Ryle reacted against this paradigm. He characterised the idea that there should exist a certain thinking device, which did not belong to the world, as "the ghost in the machine" paradigm. As a result of his criticism, Ryle concluded that knowledge cannot primarily be understood as knowledge of something. With his famous statement in *The Concept of Mind* "knowing-that" presupposes "knowing-how" (Ryle 1949). In order to know that something is the case, one must know the conditions on which it is the case. Facts are not simply facts, but they are facts according to an attitude or a point of view, which could be otherwise. The innocence of pure knowledge has been lost.

With his critique of pure knowledge and with his addition of knowing-how to knowing-that, Ryle broke the curse of knowledge. Knowledge is more than knowing-that. He passed from first order to second order knowledge. i.e. from simple knowledge (knowledge of something) to recursive knowledge (knowledge of knowledge). However, he did not reach the third or fourth orders of knowledge, i.e. the orders of knowledge in which the mystery of knowledge occurs: The orders in which new knowledge is created.

Recently, Claus Otto Scharmer has suggested that within knowledge management theories in addition to talking about explicit knowledge, which equals certified knowledge, one should include two additional categories: "processual" knowledge and "emerging" knowledge (Scharmer 2001). Furthermore, the French philosopher Michel Serres has argued that it is not sufficient just to develop a categorisation of knowledge dimensions. No, the very "nature" of knowledge should be reconsidered. Knowledge cannot be understood as a fixed, centripetal field, such as it is assumed in the encyclopaedic tradition, in which one aimed at creating a finite, universal and all-inclusive file of knowledge. No, knowledge has to be understood as an unlimited, growing and dynamic polycentric system (cf. Serres 1997 [1991]).

Definition of Knowledge

However, before developing a system of categories of knowledge one has to suggest a definition of knowledge *per se*. What is knowledge?

For me, a very simple, yet practical and applicable sociological definition of knowledge is that knowledge is confirmed observations. Observations may be confirmed over time or in society. When I observe something and then repeat my observation with the same result it becomes a confirmed observation and thus: personal knowledge. Similarly, when I observe something and another person can confirm this observation it becomes social knowledge.[1]

This implies that knowledge is not a quality of the world, but a quality of observing the world. Knowledge isn't something that we find "out there", but something that is created by observing the world and by comparing world observations over time and among different observers, bearing in mind, of course, that the observer is part of the observed world (cf. von Foerster 1984). Thus, knowledge isn't created and re-created from moment to moment, but is always a matter of confirmation of observations through repeated self-observations and through communication of others' observations. Thus, although being relatively stable, knowledge systems are always dynamic and self-developing, and different mechanisms have been created to establish such stable, but dynamic systems. The mass media system is one such system, which from day to day confirms, modifies and challenges "yesterday's knowledge". One might even suggest that so-called consensus is the contingent result of mass media mediated knowledge production. The scientific system is another knowledge producing functional system in society. The scientific system has developed very explicit and specific criteria for knowledge production, i.e. for the confirmation of observations (so-called truth criteria) and – consequently – for what counts as scientifically confirmed knowledge.

Consequently, knowledge may change over time or between social systems: Knowledge of one society or organisation may be different from the knowledge of another society or organisation. For instance our current knowledge about the system of planets is different from the knowledge of the system of planets in a traditional, pre-modern society. *We* know that the sun is the centre of the planetary system, and that the

---

1. Through the process of confirming observations, as a matter of fact observations are condensed: Many observational operations are condensed into one operation, and this operation can be called: Knowledge. This is the way in which knowledge is defined by Niklas Luhmann, who suggests "...Wissen als Kondensierung von Beobachtungen zu bezeichnen." (Luhmann 1990 p. 123)

universe is expanding. 800 years ago *"they"* knew that the earth was the centre of the planetary system, and that the universe had a fixed size, surrounded by a transparent shell with stars. In 200 years from now, yet new series of observations will have been condensed and transformed into knowledge. Thus, knowledge is contextual, which explains why knowledge sharing is not just a question of transmitting facts, but is also a question about the negotiation of a shared knowledge context.

Knowledge, then, is defined as confirmed observations. However, knowledge does not only concern observations. It also concerns actions. One may also confirm one's actions: If I do this or that, I know what will happen, because prior to the present situation this very action has been repeated by myself or by others with the same result. This type of knowledge might be termed "practical knowledge", or in the tradition of Polanyi: Tacit knowledge. I would however suggest that it is named: Skills. Skills are confirmed actions. Together, skills and knowledge constitute the totality of abilities.

One of the important implications of this definition of knowledge is that knowledge is always reflective. The knowing subject is not excluded from the extended world – the "res extensa" – but is always already included in this world. Consequently, knowledge is always both knowledge about something in the world and knowledge about itself. I fully agree with Ryle in emphasising that knowledge includes both knowing-that and knowing-how. One must always ask how one's knowledge about something is constituted the way it is.

This implies that knowledge is dynamic, and that the "dynamics" of knowledge has two sources: firstly knowledge may change, because the world changes. But secondly knowledge may change, because the way in which we observe the world changes. Furthermore, these two sources of change are interconnected: The observing or acting subject is him- or herself part of a changing world. As we shall soon see, this constitutes the theory of the categories of knowledge. Adding to know-that and know-how, one must also consider *why* our knowledge is, as it is. We know what we know according to collective paradigms of knowledge, and again these paradigms change over time (cf. Kuhn 1967). Finally, one must consider the totality of what is known and can currently be known, i.e. our knowledge culture or knowledge horizon. Inspired by Gregory Bateson, this fourth form of knowledge can be characterised as an evolutionary fact.

Function of Knowledge

Knowledge can be defined as confirmed observations. But what is the function of knowledge? Why is knowledge developed?

Here, I would suggest an evolutionary approach. I understand the development of knowledge as a special case of the general "Morphogenese von Komplexität" (Luhmann 1997 p. 415).

The basic hypothesis is that human beings and social systems survive and develop by reproducing the distinction between system and environment, that is by managing external complexity. But external complexity can only be managed through the development of internal complexity, cf. the general statement that "[o]nly complexity can reduce complexity" (Luhmann 1995 p. 26, [1984 p. 49]).

Thus, for me knowledge is a certain form of internal complexity. It is the sum of confirmed observations. According to this functional definition knowledge is a resource of all meaning-based systems, i.e. both psychic and social systems. The function of knowledge is to manage complexity.[2] Of course, in order to accumulate knowledge, other resources must be used (or developed), such as books, libraries, files etc. of the social system, and such as neural media of the psychic system. However, one does not find knowledge "in" books and files, or "in" the neurons (if this were the case, we would be back in an essential definition of knowledge), but structural couplings must be exercised between the psychic system and the brain, and between the social system and books, libraries etc.

According to the classical epistemology, a clear distinction could be made between the internal system of knowledge and the environment. According to this epistemology, the accumulation of knowledge could be understood as a closed and finite process, which happened during the "formative years" and primarily within the educational system. Here, according to this understanding, a fixed knowledge system was being built. This understanding has informed the industrial society, in which skills were accumulated through externally stimulated learning. This constitutes the learning-to-know paradigm.

However, according to a post-Cartesian epistemology, knowledge must be applied not only to the environment, but also to itself.

---

2. Cf. Nico Stehr who emphasizes that knowledge is a model *for* reality, not a model *of* reality (Stehr 2006 p. 31)

Knowledge is used in order to manage external complexity, but it is also and simultaneously used in order to manage its own complexity, i.e. to manage "eigen-complexity". Thus, the system of knowledge is characterised by not only being complex, but by being hypercomplex (cf. Qvortrup 2003). Knowledge is not a stable resource, but a dynamic, self-developing resource, constituting the learning-to-learn paradigm, and confirming the well-known sentence: The more we know, the more we know that we do not know.[3]

Categories of Knowledge

Inspired by the phenomenological critique of the Cartesian paradigm, and particularly influenced by the American anthropologist and epistemologist Gregory Bateson, in my book, *The Knowing Society*, with the subtitle: "The mystery of knowledge, learning and culture" (Qvortrup 2004) I have systematised the categories of knowledge with a special focus on the third category of knowledge, creative knowledge.

In accordance with Ryle's critique of Cartesian dualism, in the 1960s Bateson suggested that learning and communication can be divided into four categories: first, second, third and fourth order learning (Bateson 2000 [1972])[4]. Taking inspiration in Bateson's categorisation, from a post-Cartesian or – more specifically – a systems theoretical approach one can identify four forms of knowledge. First order knowledge is simple knowledge: Knowledge about something. Second order knowledge is knowledge about knowledge, i.e. recursive or situative knowledge. This category corresponds to Ryle's "knowing-how". Third order knowledge is knowledge about knowledge about knowledge, i.e. knowledge about the preconditions for recursive knowledge. Finally, one can identify a fourth category of knowledge, which represents the social evolution of knowledge, i.e. the collective and perhaps unconscious knowledge process and the total knowledge potential. This is closely related to what Edmund Husserl called the meaning horizon of society.

The theory presented in *The Knowing Society* builds on this idea. Its main claim is that a mundanised subject observing the world in order

---

3. Concerning the dynamism of knowledge see: Serres 1997.
4. See also the detailed review of Bateson's categories of learning in Qvortrup 2001.

to know about the world – and all subjects are mundanised subjects – must make the following forms of observation:

- it must observe the world as an object of observation
- it must observe itself in the world
- it must observe the world (including itself) as a precondition for observing the world.

In addition, this theory of knowledge presupposes that the world, including the subjects observing the world, exists as a knowledge horizon, i.e. as a totality of what can be known. The theory furthermore presupposes that this world is dynamic, i.e. that it changes in unforeseen directions (this is the result of its hypercomplexity, cf. Qvortrup 2003) and thus makes change of knowledge possible. It isn't just a knowledge world, but also a knowing world. Society can not adequately be characterised as a "knowledge society", but it should be termed a "knowing society". Finally, the theory assumes that changes in the world take place by virtue of the world itself. Drawing a distinction between the subject and the world, the mundanised subject changes the world through its observation, and it is changed by the world through its observation: It transforms the world and is transformed thereby, whether this last change is called socialisation or learning.

This implies that the above mentioned four categories of knowledge can be identified:

Knowledge category	Knowledge form	Knowledge designation
1st order or simple knowledge	Knowledge about something	Factual or object knowledge
2nd order or complex knowledge	Knowledge about the conditions of knowing	Recursive or situative knowledge
3rd order or hyper-complex knowledge	Knowledge about the conditions of knowledge and recursive knowledge	Reflective or creative knowledge
4th order knowledge	World knowledge or the knowledge horizon	Evolutionary or world knowledge

Where the first forms of knowledge represent observation-based forms of knowledge, i.e. relations between subject and world (including the subject's knowledge of itself as a subject in the world), the fourth form of knowledge is not knowledge about the world but the world as knowledge.

- First order knowledge is knowledge about something. For instance, I know that from where I am sitting I can see a beautiful bed of rhododendrons, and I know that the large plant in the middle is a Rhododendron Cawtabiensis.
- Second order knowledge is knowledge about knowledge, i.e. the capacity for self-observation. It is called "recursive knowledge", because it is knowledge applied to itself, and "situative knowledge", because it is the ability to use knowledge in specific situations. Often, this is called *competence*. Not only do I know that the shrub out there is a Rhododendron Cawtabiensis, but I also know that I know it because I had to elaborate my wishes to the owner of the nursery I bought it from. I also know that the fact that I consider it beautiful may be because I planted it myself. In other words, I am not only capable of categorising what I see, but I also have the ability to stand next to my own observation and consider it.
- Third order knowledge is knowledge about knowledge about knowledge, i.e. knowledge about the system of knowledge that first order knowledge is based on. It is called reflective knowledge, because it is knowledge about how to reflect the normally hidden assumptions of common knowledge. Often, this is called creativity, because it is the ability to change the assumptions or the "schemata" behind common knowledge. I know what I know according to a knowledge system or paradigm. It can, for instance, be knowledge of the botanical systematics, which lead to the designations of species that I employ. Or it can be knowledge of the aesthetic criteria for beauty, which make me find my garden beautiful. My aesthetic preferences could be caused by a predilection for English garden aesthetics rather than the more formal French or Italian classicist garden aesthetics.
- Finally, fourth order knowledge is knowledge transcending the preconditions for the knowledge systematic, i.e. the totality of knowledge as an evolutionary fact. One sometimes says that it is

represented by the entire cultural system, into which these knowledge forms and judgements of taste are embedded. Following Bateson's categories of learning and communication, this fourth order knowledge is a very particular form of knowledge, which cannot be contained within one person but resides in the social community of which the individuals are members.

The ideal knowledge worker is a worker who includes all four categories in one individual person: Firstly, he/she has accumulated a large number of confirmed observations and actions into files of factual knowledge. He or she is *qualified*. Secondly, he/she is able to improvise, to organise his/her own work together with others. He/she knows how to use his/her knowledge. He or she is *competent*. Thirdly, he/she is able to go beyond the taken-for-granted assumptions. He/she knows what constitutes his/her knowledge categories. He or she is *creative*. And finally, he/she knows that his/her and others' knowledge sum up to a knowledge system, which constitutes their common knowledge culture. He or she is *cultivated* in the sense that he/she knows that his/her knowledge is one element of an evolutionary and contingent knowledge system.

Adding to these four knowledge categories a distinction should be made between codified and non-codified knowledge, or between skills and knowledge. Skills can be defined as tacit abilities, while knowledge can be defined as codified abilities. Again, however, skills can be divided into four categories:

- ready-at-hand skills (the simple ability to e.g. use a hammer);
- situative skills (the ability to solve problems by using an instrument, e.g. using a hammer as a bottle opener);
- creative or reflective skills (the ability to practically reflect on the use of e.g. different tools, which can be found among skilled practitioners);
- the culture of skills (which is established in a workshop with different specialities, e.g. in an orchestra with specialised musicians).

The total system of abilities, divided into skills and knowledge forms, looks like this:

Forms of connaissance/skills	Forms of savoir/knowledge
Ready-at-hand skills	Factual knowledge
Situative skills	Situative knowledge
Creative skills	Creative knowledge
The culture of skills	The culture of knowledge

Knowledge Categories: The Case of ECCO Footwear

Let me illustrate the knowledge categories presented above by referring to one of the modern, knowledge-based enterprises in Denmark, ECCO Footwear. ECCO Footwear started in the 1960s as a footwear production enterprise in Denmark, employing hundreds of unskilled industrial workers. Currently, however, footwear is only designed and the total, global footwear production system is managed in Denmark, while the physical production of footwear is performed at factories in China, Indonesia and elsewhere. Consequently, within a Danish perspective, the ECCO Footwear company is a typical, knowledge-based enterprise.

What skills must those employed at a knowledge-heavy company such as ECCO Footwear possess? It would be easy to follow Richard Florida in saying that they should be "creative" workers. But although I agree with Florida, when he says that the concept of creative workers "...has a good deal more precision than existing, more amorphous definitions of knowledge workers, symbolic analysts or professional and technical workers" (Florida 2004 p. 9), not only is his category of creative workers too narrow; his rather romantic idea of creativity as something emerging from social and cultural diversity is not appropriate. Yes, creativity is part of the competencies of an employee at ECCO Footwear, but there is more to it than just creativity. Here, the categories – and the systematics – presented above can prove their usefulness.

Employees at a knowledge-heavy company such as ECCO Footwear must have considerable *factual knowledge*, i.e. a whole series of technical and professional qualifications: Designers at ECCO have to have design knowledge, knowledge of materials, and be able to use advanced digital tools.

They must have considerable recursive or *situative knowledge*. They must be able to work in teams, to handle unexpected situations with their colleagues, to improvise and empathise. They must know how to use their factual knowledge. They must be competent.

They must have reflective or *creative knowledge*. They must constantly be able to rise above the I-you situation of the group and see things from the outside, identifying and re-interpreting even basic assumptions that are perhaps not so self-evident as they appear at first glance. This is a prerequisite for being able to act creatively: to be able – taking the design and production of footwear as an example – to understand that shoes are not just shoes but narratives about and self-stagings of the person wearing them. One is not designing a functional technology but a culture-historically based tool for identity-construction and -reflection.

Lastly, they must be part of what I have referred to as *metasystemic knowledge*, or *knowledge culture*. For instance, they must be able to adopt an attitude towards the company culture of which they are a part, yet only can play a role in and contribute to by being different: the value of modern knowledge workers presupposes that they contribute to the organisation by being different. They are included by being exclusive.

2. Categories of Learning and Teaching

Teaching and Learning

"Die Absicht zu erziehen ist vor allem an Handlungen erkennbar, mit denen der Erzieher versucht, Wissen und Können an jemanden zu vermitteln, der darüber noch nicht verfügt." (Luhmann 2002 p. 59). The aim to educate is observable in actions with which the educator tries to mediate knowledge and abilities to somebody, who does not yet possess this.

But how do the parties involved – the educator and the student – fulfil this aim?

In order to answer this question at least four aspects must be addressed.

The first aspect is that a distinction must be made between teaching and learning. While teaching is restricted to communication, the learning of the students – the building of knowledge – can be defined as their own cognitive accumulation of confirmed observations. Knowledge cannot be transferred from the teacher to the student, but the teacher must select communicative actions, which can be observed by the students. The hidden mystery of education is that this observation of communicative actions (speaking, drawing on the blackboard, showing examples, etc.) in some way must be supposed to support the learning – the cognitive accumulation of confirmed observations – of the student, although the relationship between teacher and student is characterised by its double contingency.

This leads to the second implication, namely that all teaching is mediated. There is no such thing as un-mediated teaching. Also by acting, pointing, speaking and drawing, media are employed, and new digital media – computers and networks – are just new distribution media for the specialised communication of teaching.

Thirdly, learning – the dynamic accumulation of confirmed observations and the resulting accommodation of the existing knowledge scheme – cannot be directly observed. The teacher cannot observe whether or what the student learns. He or she can only observe the indirect expressions of the learning process, for instance by asking the student to join the educational communication process. This can be done in the informal discussions in the classroom or in formal test settings. However, the aim is the same: To achieve some indirect sign of the learning of the pupil.

Finally, the fourth point – or assumption – is that there is a connection between forms of teaching and forms of knowledge. In order to mediate certain forms of knowledge adequate forms of teaching should be selected.

Categories of Learning and Teaching

It is my research-based hypothesis that there is a connection between the four categories of knowledge and corresponding categories of learning and learning stimulation, i.e. teaching. This does not imply that one type of knowledge only corresponds to one type of learning, and that it can only be mediated through one type of teaching (or, with a more precise concept, learning stimulation). But the assumption is that one form of teaching is better aimed at mediating the accumulation of one particular form of knowledge than other forms of teaching.

Thus, in order to mediate 1st order learning – accumulation of confirmed observations i.e. 1st order knowledge processes – direct learning stimulation through classroom teaching, lecturing etc. is adequate.

The assumption is that this can be represented by a first order equation, where there is a one-to-one correspondence between input and output. As can be seen in the illustration, there is a first-order equation correspondence between this type of teaching and learning. However, over time the teaching-learning factor – the so-called "learning curve" – can be increased:

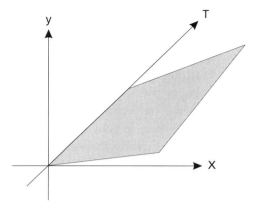

In order to mediate 2nd order learning, i.e. construction of knowledge concerning how to use one's abilities in an adequate way for solving tasks and problems, stimulation of self-learning is adequate. This is practised through group work, project work etc. Inspired by Jean Piaget, this learning type might be called assimilation.

The assumption is that this type of learning can be represented by a second order equation, because the acquirement of one task solving competence results in the ability to solve not one, but two or four problems:

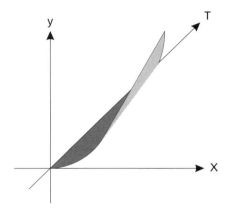

The 3rd category of knowledge is knowledge about the conditions of knowledge, and having knowledge about the conditioning of common knowledge it the precondition for changing these conditions. Again inspired by Piaget the corresponding learning form might be called: Accommodation. When somebody accommodates, he or she changes the structure of knowledge, i.e. the basic assumptions. This is typically practised in creative teaching environments, for instance at the higher classes of art schools, where the student is supposed – and is stimulated – to create his or her own "style". But it is also practised in the process of writing master theses, in which the student is supposed to discuss and even to challenge existing theoretical assumptions.

Here, it is the assumption that this type of learning can be represented by a third order equation, in which under certain condition the input-output relation turns upside-down in the sense that a certain input results in an opposite output, cf. René Thom's theory of catastrophes (cf. Thom 1975 and 1983):

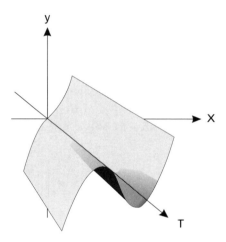

Finally, the fourth form of learning is about the total learning topology, be it a finite curriculum process, the total process of a person's lifelong learning or the learning of an organisation or a society. Here, one does not just learn to learn (which is what happens in the 2nd and 3rd forms of learning), but one is part of a lifelong and collective learning process. Such processes can be stimulated in educational planning, but also in creating the architectural context of the learning processes in educational institutions. To build a school or to plan the total curriculum is to act at the order of fourth order learning stimulation.

In schematic form, these categories and correspondences can be summarised as follows, again emphasising that there is no simple or causal relationship between one category and the other.

1. order learning	Accumulation	Qualifications	Direct learning stimulation (class room teaching, lecturing)
2. order learning	Assimilation	Competencies	Stimulation of self-learning (group and project work)
3. order learning	Accommodation	Creativity	Stimulation of self-conditioning (construction of learning conditions)
4. order learning	Change of paradigm	Culture	Change of social and organisational conditions (...of basic conditions)

Curriculum planning

One of the most obvious implications of the theory of knowledge categories is that it can inform curriculum planning. The idea is that any curriculum must be structured according to the knowledge categories, and that adequate teaching forms must be chosen.

Let me illustrate this idea by the case of history. A history course must be based on 1st order knowledge, that is on historical facts. Having a course of Danish history the students must learn that the Danish king Christian IV built a number of the most important and beautiful buildings in Copenhagen, buildings that still are providing cultural identity to the city. Having a course of the Middle East and the Arab world, students should know that the present day state of Iraq was defined in 1919 by The United Kingdom as a patchwork of different Islamic cultures and of parts of Kurdistan. Here, a combination of reading and lecturing seems to be an adequate teaching method.

However, this accumulation of 1st order knowledge should lead into development of 2nd order knowledge. i.e. knowledge answering the question concerning the use – and usefulness – of 1st order knowledge. Here, the students are not primarily accumulating facts, but they place themselves in an observation position outside the basic facts, asking what they can be used for. Concerning the course of Danish history the knowledge of who created the basic buildings of Copenhagen could lead into considerations concerning the cultural identity of the city and of the layout of its fundamental geographical power structure. Concerning the course of Iraq, the knowledge of the post 1st World War nation design could of course inform the understanding of the current problems of establishing a stable, post-dictatorship Iraq. Here, is seems adequate to include project work, class-room discussions and other forms of more independent individual or group based student work, thus stimulating the development of competencies, i.e. the ability to use the basic factual qualifications for problem solving.

Going into 3rd order knowledge would imply that for instance theories and paradigms should be explicitly included in the teaching. Here the students should not only observe their primary factual knowledge from a pragmatic point of view, asking what it can be used for, but they should observe the way in which observations are made. Why does the historical world look in one way, and not in other ways? Why is the choice of an initial distinction – leading into a paradigm of concepts – important for the way in which facts appear for the observer? In the case of the Danish history of course the classical question would be: Did Christian IV really build these buildings? Wasn't it the workers who were forced to do so? Or, equally importantly: Who actually designed these buildings? The students would learn that the current city of Copenhagen is influenced by French architectural design, and thus that Copenhagen isn't a pure "Danish" city, but is an amalgamation of cultural influences from Germany, France and Italy. But they would also learn that things are not, what they appear to be. Facts are always seen through a paradigm or an "optical design", which could be different. They learn to observe their own observations and thus to understand that if they put themselves into another observational position, they might come to a different result. They learn to be creative. Here, it seems adequate to include broad classroom discussions, asking students to present different approaches to the subject.

Finally, 4th order knowledge is knowledge about the totality of knowledge as an evolutionary fact, i.e. knowledge about society as a dynamic knowledge horizon. The students should understand that there are limits for understanding, that certain horizons condition our knowledge of the world as what would earlier be called a matter of transcendentality. How can this be illustrated in the history class? One way of doing so would be to discuss our history as a cultural horizon. The reference to King Christian IV is a reference to a collective reference point and thus a reference to one or the millions of facts that constitute a common cultural identity. Thus, history is part of all that knowledge, which constitutes a horizon of knowledge that defines Danes as Danes.

With this example I want to illustrate the way in which the categories of knowledge can inform the curriculum planning and the teaching practice. I certainly do not suggest that a linear structure should be made from 1st to 4th order knowledge, nor do I suggest that every student independently of age and abilities can work equally well with all knowledge forms. But I suggest that both the curriculum planning and the teaching practice should be based on the inclusion of all knowledge forms, that every subject should be seen within all knowledge contexts, and that teaching and working forms should be selected in accordance with those forms of learning that are related to the actual knowledge form.

Categories of Evaluation

The learning of the student cannot be directly observed by the teacher. There is no introspective tool or trick allowing the teacher to observe the learning process. He or she can only observe those communicative utterances which may (or may not) be an expression of what the student has understood and learned. In order to do so, different communication tricks can be used, from the discussions in the classroom over the observations of the students ("are they committed?", "do they follow me?" etc.) to the formal organisation of communicative evaluation events in tests and examinations.

It is my hypothesis that there is a correspondence between different knowledge forms and evaluation forms.

The traditional examination, which tests the acquirement of factual knowledge, can be organised as a summative evaluation, for instance as a multiple-choice test. Here, the function of the evaluation is to observe whether the student has accumulated knowledge according to the requirements presented in the curriculum.

Other knowledge forms however call for other evaluation forms. If one wants to test whether second order knowledge has been acquired, e.g. whether a problem-oriented project group has learned how to solve problems, a group examination should be organised, focusing on the ability to solve problems, i.e. work together, create problem solving strategies etc. Here, the observation of the examiner must be oriented not only towards the accumulated knowledge, but also towards the knowledge development strategies acquired by the members of the project group. As these competencies point towards the future ability to solve comparable problems, this evaluation form can be called: formative evaluation.

Focusing on third order knowledge, it is my assumption that indirect of meta-reflective evaluation forms should be used. How does one find out whether a work of art produced by an art student is good or bad? In order to do so, one must include the discussion of evaluation criteria, that is organise what could be called systemic evaluation. Here, the evaluation criteria are included in the evaluation process as part of the discussion. Taking the example of an art student examination, the work of art cannot be tested as simply correct of incorrect. The examiner necessarily has to discuss with the art student, which aesthetic criteria he or she finds valuable, and in which ways the work of art is related to these specific aesthetic criteria. The same meta-reflective approach can be found in e.g. the evaluation of a master or PhD thesis, where it is necessary to write an evaluation report. A single mark or grade is not sufficient, because it cannot include the reflection of the criteria for the evaluation.

Finally, the total system of evaluations constitutes an evaluation culture, which can be found in e.g. organisational procedures of ongoing self-evaluation. An organization that continuously evaluates itself has established an evaluation culture, i.e. a fourth order knowledge oriented evaluation form.

Knowledge form	Evaluation form
Factual knowledge ("qualifications")	Summative evaluation
Recursive knowledge ("competencies")	Formative evaluation
Reflective knowledge ("creativity")	Systemic evaluation (evaluation of evaluation)
Metareflective knowledge ("culture")	Evaluation and self-evaluation culture

The reflective Teacher

Inspired by Donald Schön's classic book from 1983 *The Reflective Practitioner* (Schön 1991), in which he analyses the ways in which professionals think in action, i.e. reflect on their ongoing professional activity, one can identify different forms of teaching reflection.

The basic form is what could be phrased basic teaching practices. The teacher communicates with the class of students in order to stimulate their learning processes.

In his classical analysis of communication, Paul Watzlawick demonstrated that one cannot just communicate. All communication implies communication about communication or observation of communication. When we communicate, we observe the way in which the other communicates and the way we communicate ourselves: Why didn't he make eye contact when he complimented me? How should I respond appropriately? Literary speaking, the communicator is divided into two persons: One who communicates, and one who observes the ongoing communication (Watzlawick et al. 1968).

Similarly, teaching practice is always combined with an ongoing reflection on teaching. However, using the categories of knowledge this reflection and self-reflection activity can be specified.

The basic form of teaching self-reflection is observation of the teaching practice. Of course the teacher has to observe the students in order to get an idea of their learning activity, but simultaneously he will also observe his own teaching as communication in order to reflect whether the utterances chosen are appropriate or not. In its formalised form this type of teaching reflection can be named didactics, assuming that didactics can be defined as that form of teaching reflection that is related to a specific topic or to a specific teaching practice. Didactics is the methodology of teaching.

In addition to teaching reflection comes what can be called educational meta-reflection. Here the teacher includes reflection about the values and assumptions of the basic process of teaching and reflection. Implicitly or explicitly he discusses on which assumptions the immediate teaching and teaching reflection is based. This second order teaching reflection can be phrased pedagogy, assuming that pedagogy is theoretically formalised reflection about teaching and teaching reflection, including the basic assumptions and values of teaching. Pedagogy is the theory of teaching.

Finally the organisation of a group of teachers, including their mutual discussions about teaching practices and mutual teaching observations, for instance in teacher teams, is equal to the fourth category of teaching reflection: The teaching, reflection and meta-reflection culture of an organisation, for instance of a school, i.e. the totality of the teachers' practices and their methodological and theoretical discussions.

Knowledge form	Evaluation form
Factual knowledge ("qualifications")	Teaching practice
Recursive knowledge ("competencies")	Teaching reflection: Didactics
Reflective knowledge ("creativity")	Teaching meta-reflection: Pedagogy
Metareflective knowledge ("culture")	Teaching culture/organisation

Conclusion

In these first two chapters I have argued that in order to develop a theory of the so-called "Knowledge Society" – or as I prefer: "The Knowing Society" – it is necessary to create an explicit definition of knowledge and a systematic theory of knowledge forms.

According to my theory, four categories – or four reflection levels – of knowledge can be identified. 1st order knowledge, or factual knowledge, results from the immediate observation of facts. The accumulation of 1st order knowledge is a simple, summative activity. 2nd order knowledge, or recursive knowledge, results from the recursive observation of factual knowledge. This is aimed at developing competencies, i.e. abilities to solve problems with one's factual knowledge. 3rd order knowledge, or reflective knowledge, results from the reflection of the combination of qualifications and competencies: What lies behind the way in which I observe things, and the way in which I solve problems? This 3rd order knowledge is about the – often hidden – basic assumptions of our knowledge-based practices. Knowing about basic assumptions makes it possible to modify or change these basic assumption and thus to be creative. Finally, 4th order knowledge is the evolution of world knowledge, be it the total knowledge of interaction groups, organisations or societies. 4th order knowledge – world knowledge – represents the totality of what is known and what can currently be known.

Based on these categories of knowledge, four categories of learning can be identified, leading into a better understanding of teaching forms and of evaluation forms. Also, four corresponding forms of the reflective teacher's self-reflection can be identified.

The final aim of these theoretical efforts is to contribute to the development of a theoretical basis for educating the professional teacher, assuming that the days have past when teaching was an activity based only on common sense. In a knowledge society teaching is a professional activity founded on research-based evidence.

3. Media Pedagogy:

Media Education, Media Socialisation and Educational Media

Introduction

Until now I have analysed the basic concepts: knowledge, learning and teaching. But teaching and education could not happen without media. When I lecture, I speak to a group of students, using the spoken language as my primary medium. But I also gesture, walk around, make drawings on the blackboard, involve one or two students in discussions in order to address the issue in other ways, and sometimes even use Powerpoint slides in order to illustrate my case. Getting back to my office, I communicate with the students through our learning management system, Blackboard, downloading the slides from the lecture and commenting on results from a teamwork session.

But not only do I communicate through media, I also try to address the fact that students are used to living in an environment of digital media. They have there own websites, they blog, they expect last minute changes to be communicated as sms messages. And as a matter of fact my lecture is about media and culture. Thus, media isn't just the means but also the subject of the lecture.

Consequently, the aim of this chapter is to examine the relationship between education and media. These two concepts can be combined in three ways: one can think of media education, i.e. education in the subject of mass media. One can think of media socialisation, i.e. education within the context of a media society in which pupils and students are experienced media users. Finally, one can think of educational media, i.e. media used for educational purposes.

After having specified these three subject areas, the chapter focuses on the third subject: Media used for educational purposes. According to the chapter, teaching can be defined as a specialised form of communication, and the basic point of the chapter is that all communication is mediated. One cannot talk about such a thing as "non-mediated" communication. Also talking or touching implies media: Verbal or body language.

Consequently, the introduction of new, digital media for teaching does not imply that teaching is made more artificial or non-authentic. The introduction of new, digital media for teaching only implies that other and older educational media are re-mediated.

Pedagogy and Didactics

The present chapter is about media pedagogy and media didactics. Thus, as an introduction, I should specify the way in which I define the key concepts of pedagogy and didactics.

Pedagogy is defined as the theory of education, i.e. the theory of the way in which external influence – teaching and upbringing – can change the object of this influence. In comparison, didactics is defined as the methodology of education. This implies that the definition of these concepts is based on the position of the observer in relation to the phenomenon of teaching. Didactics is first order reflection of teaching, while pedagogy is second order reflection (cf. chapter two).

Thus, for me, the difference between pedagogy and didactics is the following: According to my definition didactics can be understood as reflection of practice, i.e. reflection concerning the way in which the teacher can realise his or her educational objective. Thus, didactics is the theory of the teacher as reflective practitioner (cf. Schön 1991 [1983]) specialised in education. In comparison, pedagogy is the theory of second order educational reflection, i.e. reflection concerning the unity of education and reflection of education. The subject of pedagogy is educational theory, while the subject of didactics is educational methodology.

Media Pedagogy

What happens, when the word "media" is combined with the word "pedagogy", i.e. when one talks about "media pedagogy"? Three things can happen. One possibility is that "media pedagogy" means that special kind of educational theory focusing on media teaching and media training. If this is the case, media pedagogy can be compared with literature pedagogy, language pedagogy, pedagogy of physics, chemistry, natural sciences, music, art, etc.

Another possibility is that "media pedagogy" means that special kind of educational theory, which focuses on teaching and upbringing in a media society. What happens to education, when pupils and students are experienced users of media? Should the teacher teach differently in this social context, for instance by training the students not to be influenced by mass media, and does the socialisation in a media society condition teaching differently, for instance by making children better informed and/or more impatient? They read books – cf. the Harry Potter phenomenon – watch television, play computer games, surf the Internet, listen to i-pod music, send and receive sms's, talk in mobile telephones, etc. etc.

The third possibility is that the word combination "media pedagogy" means that specialised part of pedagogy, which deals with the use and role of media in education. When a teacher teaches, he or she uses media. Language for talking, blackboards for writing, body language for creating direct communicational contact – and computers, digital networks, Learning Management Systems, etc.

Thus, "media pedagogy" can be interpreted in three ways:

– The first possible meaning is the theory of media education. How does one teach the pupils and students to use media, and how does one teach them about media as a phenomenon in society? This may be called the theory of *media education.*
– The second possible meaning is the theory of education under those special conditions that mass media represent a special aspect of socialisation in relation to the pupils. Pupils know the world through the media, and they are experienced and competent media users. This may be called the theory of education of media socialised children, or – in brief – the theory of *media socialisation.*
– The third possible meaning is the theory of education by means of media: How are media used in and for teaching, from body and verbal language in the classroom over school radio and school television to e-learning, e-portfolio and Learning Management Systems. This may be called the theory of *educational media.*

Thus, "media pedagogy" is the theory of education about media, it is the theory of education within the context of media and media society, and it is the theory of education with media. In the following, I will outline all these possibilities. However, I will not hide the fact that I am particularly interested in the third point: How can dissemination media be used in and for teaching?

I will however emphasise my first point of the present chapter: That it is important to make a distinction between these three ways of interpreting the concept of "media pedagogy". Much too often these three definitions are being mixed together.

Media Education

What makes media education different from all other education? Is teaching media basically different from teaching Danish, Spanish, mathematics, physics etc.?

For me the basic difference is more than the difference concerning subject. For me the objective is different. If one teaches Danish, Spanish or mathematics, the objective is that the students should learn these subjects. But the objective of media education is to teach the students to deal with communication and dissemination media as producers and as users, and to become citizens in a so-called media society.

In this respect media education is much more directly related to the basic dilemma of modern education – some call it the paradox of education – that the basic aim of education is through teaching to influence the students not to be susceptible to influence (cf. von Oettingen 2002). The dilemma of education is through communicative influences to make children free citizens. This is of course the teleological dilemma of all education. But in media education this is very present in the curriculum. Here, teachers use media to influence students in order not to be susceptible to mediatised influence. Here, teachers aim to make students interested in media, while simultaneously teaching them to distance themselves from the influence of media.

Sometimes, the administration of this dilemma has been called "housewife research" (cf. Fritze, Haugsbakk and Nordkvelle 2004 pp. 206-214). On the one hand one tries to prevent children from what is seen as the harmful influence of media, on the other hand one introduces children to the fascinating world of mass media. What is the objective of teaching computer games? Is it to prevent children from playing computer games, or is it to support their game abilities and aesthetic competencies in relation to computer games? As I have suggested, this dilemma is not unique for media education, but it represents a general pedagogical dilemma. However, the dilemma is particularly obvious in media education.

Sometimes, the dilemma is managed by simply choosing a particular position. Then, the objective of media education is – as it is often expressed – to turn children into "critical media consumers". They should not be become "victims" of newspaper advertisements, television commercials or Internet banners, but should be able to see through the tricks by learning their communicative effects. Commercials should not be loved, but unmasked.

In this respect media education is different from other school subjects. The objective of mathematics is not to create critical mathematicians; the aim of literature is not to educate children to establish a critical distance to fiction writers such as Shakespeare or Hans Christian Andersen. The literature teacher does not aim at critical readings of *The Ugly Duckling,* but aims at stimulating love and fascination. But the media teacher certainly wants to stimulate critical reading of *The Sun* or *Disney* commercials, and he leaves very little room for fascination.

One way of solving this dilemma is to divide the subject into two parts: A production part and a reception part.

In the production part children are educated to be able to manage media production tools, not least computers. Here, the curriculum includes teleological as well as aesthetic elements. One should be able to use the computer in a targeted way in order to produce the result aimed at. And one should know and admire media aesthetics in order to create beautiful and fascinating products.

In the reception part children are educated in order to become sceptical media consumers. Here they do not produce media effects; here they unmask these same effects. Here they are not supposed to be fascinated, but critical.

How does one manage such dilemmas or, as they are sometimes called, paradoxes? The rational approach would suggest that dilemmas or paradoxes should be solved or "untied". But what do you do, if the paradox is a real one, i.e. if it is inextricable? Then one has to try a radically different strategy: To make the dilemma or paradox invisible. And this is exactly what the educational system does.

Niklas Luhmann expresses this approach in the following way:

> Das Erziehungssystem hat eigene Formen des Umgangs mit Paradoxen entwickelt. Es nennt sich zu diesem Zwecke "Bildungssystem". Dabei geht es vor allem darum, die Paradoxien zu entstören und sie so weit zu invisibilisieren, daß sie unbemerkt bleiben können. Oder anders gesagt: die unergiebige Kurzzeitoszillation im Paradox muß ersetzt werden durch Problemstellungen, die mit Hoffnung auf Lösung der Probleme ausgestattet sind. (Luhmann 2004d p. 241 [1996])

In a free translation Luhmann says: The educational system has developed its own ways to manage paradoxes. In this respect the educational system calls itself the system of "Bildung", i.e. of general cultivation or cultural education. The strategy is to avoid that paradoxes make too much noise, it is to make them invisible so that no attention is paid to the paradox. Or, otherwise expressed: the unpleasant short time oscillation of the paradox has to be replaced by articulations of the problem, which couch the problem in a hope for solution.

Thus, the general answer to the dilemmas or paradoxes of education is: Bildung, i.e. general cultivation or cultural education, as a communicative trick. "General cultivation" is a contingency formula,[1] which makes it possible to communicate about education as if it was not inherently paradoxical. What is the objective of education, is the question. Is it: To form children in a certain way, or is it to make them impossible to form? The answer that covers this dilemma is: Bildung.

The inherent dilemma of media education has a similar solution: "Media Bildung" or general media cultivation. This specific contingency formula covers the doubleness of fascinated media production and sceptical media reception.

---

1. This concept was introduced by Niklas Luhmann and Karl Eberhard Schorr in 1979, cf. the definition of the concept in Luhmann and Schorr 1988 pp. 58-62 [1979]. See also Luhmann 2002, pp. 183-196.

Another reaction to the problem of contingency is to suggest normative or declarative answers. Within the field of media, one illustrative example is the many cases of literacy-declarations: Media literacy, information literacy, computer literacy, network literacy, to mention only a few of the suggestions. The mechanism seems to be that some self-fancied authoritative body – even the names are illustrative: The American Library Association's Presidential Committee on Information Literacy from 1989, The National Leadership Conference on Media Literacy from 1993, etc. – expect that contingency can be neutralised by public declarations. That the problem isn't solved, but rather given yet another articulation, can be seen by simply comparing the many incompatible normative proposals.

Media Socialisation

All teaching presupposes that the teacher makes a "picture" of the pupil. If the objective of teaching is to change pupils into certain directions, i.e. to meet the aims of the curriculum and to make the students learn certain things, then the teacher must act as if the student is a simple device.

However, the teacher knows that this isn't the case. Students or pupils are not simple devices or trivial machines, but non-trivial devices. When students are influenced by the interaction of the teacher, they will react in non-foreseeable ways. "Their reaction on impulses will always be mediated through self-reference. That is: They will ask themselves what they can do with – or should understand – a certain input, and they can react on the same input in different ways at different moments." (Luhmann 2004a p. 15 [1985]. My translation LQ)

Still, however, normally the teacher will interact with the students or pupils as if they were, what they are not: Trivial devices. He asks them what two times two is, knowing that there is one correct answer, or he asks them when Homer was born, knowing that the one and only correct answer is: "That is not known" (ibid.). Translated into categories of knowledge, the teacher interacts with students as if all knowledge is factual knowledge, although it is well known that this is not the case. (Qvortrup 2004)

This, thus, represents another inherent dilemma of the educational system: That teachers interact with students as if they were trivial devices, knowing that in reality they are non-trivial devices. They communicate with students as if communication is transportation of knowledge, knowing that the basic condition of communication is double contingency: The teacher cannot observe the learning processes of the student, and the student cannot observe the intentional processes of the teacher's selection of communicative utterances.

Again, there is no easy solution to this dilemma. One would not like to – and actually could not – transform students into trivial machines (although sometimes this seems to be the implicit effect of the intentional structure of the educational system). Still, however, one wants them to learn what they have been taught.

The answer to the dilemma, that the structural coupling between the communication system of the class-room and the psychic system of the student is both necessary and impossible, is to perform yet another communicative trick, i.e. to translate the contingent human being student into what Luhmann calls a "person", that is into a communicatively accessible instance. The mechanism is that we simplify the other in order to make communication possible, while we know that by doing so we reduce the other to something that he or she is not.

This is of course even more acute, as teachers do not communicate with one student at a time, but with several students. The challenge of the teacher is not just to interact with one non-trivial device, but to interact with a non-trivial system of non-trivial devices.

Consequently, one of the activities often seen among teachers is to make general characteristics of pupils. They are characterised as "...the children of our time". To interact educationally with children in a classroom the teacher has to typify them, for instance as "competent", "narcissistic", "early matured", etc. Similarly, teachers often talk about the characteristics of a whole class: "This class is good, that other class is lazy."

In order to perform this communicative trick, the individual children must be seen as a product of a common cause. They are supposed to be "socialised". The idea of socialisation is, among other things, a trick used by teachers to categorise pupils and students under a common denominator. One can then talk about spoilt children, second-generation immigration children, working class children, academic family children etc. And one can generalise children into children belonging to certain generations: Critical generations, happy-go-lucky generations etc. Doing so, the teacher can so to speak communicate with what is believed to have conditioned the children. Instead of looking into their souls – finding nothing – they can look into their social environment.

In this respect so-called "media socialisation" is a communicative trick. It is a way of reducing children into a simple category, thus acting as if classroom teaching is possible. In order to construct the generalised communicative other, one can include him or her into the media socialised general other and act in correspondence with this generalisation. He or she can be said to having been socialised through media, and to having made his or her world experiences through media. Students of our times are "products of the media", "Disney-fied", they are "in lack of first order experience", etc.

But isn't this true? No, if it is correct that society and humans – psychic systems – are mutually closed systems, human beings are not a simple product of society. Norms, patterns, traditions etc. cannot be transmitted from one generation to the next. Rather, the mechanism of socialisation should be analysed as a mechanism of expectations (Luhmann 2004c [1987]). The child or the young person can observe the communication of the older generation, the teachers or the other young people, and he or she can react through adaptation or deviation. Should I accept their communicative offer, or shouldn't I?

This is of course also the fact at the next level of observation. The young person observes the expectations of the other, or he observes the reactions from the other on his being this or that.

In this respect socialisation is more "free" then education. Socialisation is characterised as structures of expectations, but whether the other fulfils your expectations is not important. Actually, it may be seen as positive if the other deviates from the expected outcome.

But education is goal-oriented communication. Children and students should learn something according to the curriculum, and they may react against these objectives. Therefore, as Luhmann notices, it is an old pedagogical trick to organise education as situations, which are supposed to actualise a certain socialisation potential. One might for instance identify pupils as media society children and provide them with computers, mobile telephones and treat them as experienced media practitioners – and this might then have a positive outcome in relation to the curriculum.

Educational Media

Until now I have looked at the two first aspects of media pedagogy: Media education and media socialisation. Media education is about the way in which teaching students how to use media can be organised and practised. Media socialisation is about the way in which teaching can be organised and practised, assuming that students have a common socialisation in media and in media society.

The rest of the chapter I will however devote to the third subject: How to use media in and for education. I will do so by discussing the question: What is a theory of educational media, that is a theory of teaching which has a special focus on the use and function of media in teaching?

On the face of it, one would think that this would be a theory about the special and atypical type of teaching that is performed by means of radio, television and new, digital media. Thus, this would be a theory about school-radio, school-television, distance learning, computer-supported learning, etc.

However, I would suggest that a theory about educational media should have a much broader definition. It is my hypothesis that all teaching is using media, that is, all teaching is mediated. I would like to draw a sketch of the dimensions of that particular field of pedagogy, which can be called the theory of the function of media in upbringing and teaching. I would suggest that six dimensions could be identified:

- First, I will argue that all teaching is mediated. This is the basic statement of media pedagogy.
- Second, I will describe the functionality of media in teaching as a specialised form of communication: Why are media used?
- Third, I will look at the reflectivity of educational communication. I will demonstrate that educational communication includes first order as well as second order reflection, and that educational media should make reflections at both levels possible.

- Fourth, I will analyse the basic forms of relation of education, namely the the relations between student and subject, teacher and student and teacher and subject. Each relationship calls forward a specific media type.
- Fifth, I will clarify the dimensions of educational communication, i.e. that one dimension of education is the one connecting rules and self-organisation, while the other dimension is the one connecting virtuality and reality, and I will demonstrate the way in which educational media mediate these dimensions.
- Finally, I will look at the theory of educational media from a media specific approach. I will analyse a couple of specific examples of media genres such as playgrounds and computer games in order to demonstrate the analytical potentials of the above-mentioned concepts and categories.

All teaching is mediated

It is often heard that one can make a distinction between mediated and non-mediated communication, and thus between mediated and non-mediated teaching. The idea is that there is some kind of particularly "authentic" interaction and teaching, one in which the social distance between the communicators – e.g. between teacher and student – has been eliminated. They have established an "authentic" relationship.[2]

For me, this is an illusion. All teaching – and all communication – is mediated. Also when sitting in front of the particular other in an educational relationship, this relationship is mediated. Yes, the very fact that this relationship is not any relationship, but a relationship of upbringing or teaching, represents a mediation. Also when talking to each other, verbal language, gesture etc. are media. Thus, all education, and indeed all communication, is mediated.

One could of course reply to this position that there is a marked

---

2. This position can be found in e.g. Hubert L. Dreyfus: *On the Internet* (Dreyfus 2001). See my critical discussion in the following chapter on e-learning. In Denmark the same position is articulated in Per Fibæk Laursen's book about the so-called "Authentic Teacher", cf. Laursen 2004. Within a general media scientific context this position is widespread. Here it builds on a rather narrow definition of media as technical dissemination media. See for instance Hjarvard 2005, p. 36, where he analyses the "replacement" of face-to-face communication by "mediated" communication.

difference between on the one hand language, gesture etc. and on the other hand technical media such as printed books, broadcasting programmes or e-learning systems. For me, however, it is important to emphasise that language, gesture and technical dissemination media are related. First of all, they are evolutionary related. No communication media is "authentic". Language is a product of social evolution as well as the Internet. Secondly, they are functionally related. They are means for making communication less unlikely.

This position can be substantiated as follows. Education, i.e. upbringing and teaching, is a particular form of communication, namely that form of communication whose objective is to change individuals (pupils, students, adult students) into a certain direction. More precisely, teaching is a specialised form of communication whose objective is based on a pedagogical intention to provide a person or a group of persons with knowledge and/or abilities (Rasmussen 2004 p. 11). This in itself represents a mediation. Educational communication occurs in the medium of a code, through which one can decide, whether this communicative action actually is teaching, or something else. Also, based on the code one can decide, whether the communication was successful. Did education actually happen?

Thus, just by being "education" and not conversation, negotiation, decision-making etc. the communication is mediated, because one code and not others is applied.

In addition, however, we know that the possibility for this communication to be successful is limited. When one educates a child, it is difficult to say, whether the upbringing is a result of the child's self-learning, or the result of the specific educational communication. Is the child taught to walk, or does it learn – does it teach itself – to walk? Is it taught to talk, or does it learn to talk? Here, it is relevant with Luhmann to say that teaching is a specialised expression of the general improbability that "systems understand systems" (Luhmann 2004b [1986]), i.e. that one closed system should be able to observe another closed system in such a way, that the result is understanding. Yes, it is a piece of disingenuousness to say that one psychic system observes the other. Rather, one system, i.e. the pupil, observes another system, namely the system of educational communication, personalised in communicative decisions made by a generalised other: The teacher.

In order to generalise this position, one can say – as does Luhmann in *Das Erziehungssystem der Gesellschaft*, (Luhmann 2002) – that the theory of education must make use of two basic concepts: Operative closure and structural coupling (ibid. p. 22). The concept of "operative closure" characterises both the child and the educational communication. The child is a closed system, which based on its own operations, i.e. based on preconditions that it can only create itself, observe communicative operations in its environment. My one-year-old grandchild obviously observes what I am doing and saying, but what she actually sees and understands, and why she reacts in one particular way and not another, is not observable for me. I can see *that* she observes, but I certainly cannot see *what* she sees or *why* she reacts in one way or the other. Suddenly she makes an utterance. But why did she do it now and not a month ago (actually I have said "book" hundreds of times, when she points to my shelves, without any other reply than what I interpret as "what's that?") is beyond the potentials of my understanding. Certainly, however, it is the result of her own operations and not of my utterance: Something in her makes her react.

In a similar way one can think of the educational communication as an operatively closed process, the environment of which is – children. The teacher talks, demonstrates, makes gestures and drawings on the blackboard, but whether this affects the pupils, and in which way it does so, is in principle impossible to know. And seen from the position of the children communication occurs – just think of my grandchild – but how should it be understood?

However, the result is not an absurd Leibnizian dance of isolated monads. The idea is that contact is made, but not in the sense of causal input-output processes, but in the sense of structural couplings. A "structural coupling" is a coupling made by one system and based on operations of this particular system. I observe my environment through the operations of my cognitive system, not as the environment exists "an sich". And of course I observe myself observing my environment.[3]

Structural couplings can have two different basic effects. One is that one system limits the operational potentials of the other system.

---

3. The classical conceptualisation is that of Heinz von Foerster in his book *Observing Systems* (von Foerster 1984).

Although I – and not my brain – think, in order for my cognitive system to work it must make structural couplings to the neural processes of the brain. Consequently, not everything can be seen and thought. For instance, what I can observe it limited by the visual potentials of my eye. Similarly, in order to be systematically stimulated to learn, the child must go to school. But staying at school the child is not allowed to leave the classroom, and the learning stimulation couplings are limited to what the school offers.

The other effect, which I have already indirectly mentioned, is that one system provides resources to the eigen-operations of the other system. In order to think, I must have a brain with a complex system of neural operations, but – as already said – it is not the complex system of neural operations that thinks, but "me" that do so thanks to the resources provided by my neural system. The social system communicates, but it does so thanks to the resources provided by the structurally coupled individuals – or psychic systems – in its environment. When observing the educational communication the child can observe phenomena that can be used as resources for its own operations. The small child can copy the sounds and gesture of the adult person and use this as resources for its own, continued eigen-operations.

Also in order to make structural couplings possible media must be applied. Media are so to speak the evolutionary outcome of structural couplings, and it is the function of media to make the improbability of successful communication less improbable. In the educational context media are used in order to make it more probable that the educational communication has the premeditated effect. Indeed, educational communication is mediated. We all know that we talk differently – more clear, more simple and with a more explicit orientation towards the intended effects – when we talk to a child within an educational context. However, mediation of educational communication is not an exception. On the contrary: All communication is mediated. Such a thing as unmediated communication does not exist.

Educational Media: Dissemination, Understanding and Effect

An analysis of communication, both in general terms and in relation to the special type of educational communication, implies that three types of improbability for successful communication can be identified.

Just think of the normal classroom experiences: First of all, it is not probable that the pupils should hear what is being said. Secondly, it is not probable that they understand, what is being said. Thirdly, it is not very likely that the children – if, against all odds, they have heard and understood what was said – react to what has been uttered in accordance with the intention of the communication. This can be illustrated by Luhmann's own example from the evening meal in his family. When he said to the children that they should wash their hands, they didn't hear it. They were too busy doing their own things. When they, after all, heard what he said, they didn't understand it. They looked at their hands and simply couldn't understand what was meant. "Dirty? What do you mean?" And when they finally understood it, they didn't react accordingly, but continued doing what they thought was more important, silently backed up by their gentle mother, who let the family understand that it wasn't after all *that* important.

A similar example has been provided by Søren Kierkegaard. He presented one of his ethical essays to a person, he knew – but obviously didn't admire. In the book he made the following dedication: It is not likely that you take the time to read the book. If you do so, you probably will not understand it. And even though this should be the case, you certainly will not change your lifestyle accordingly. However, he sarcastically added, I believe that you will be pleased to note that it is bound in chamois with gold-printing. Again, there are three improbabilities: The improbabilities of being heard, understood, and accepted and followed.

Based on these three types of communicative improbability, which also characterises educational communication, three types of media can be identified:[4]

— It is improbable that the child hears what the teacher says, i.e. that the message reaches the addressee. Consequently, dissemination media (writing, printing, loudspeakers, broadcasting) must be used.

---

4. The following is based on Niklas Luhmann 1995 pp. 157-163 [1984].

- It is improbable that the child understands what the teacher says. Consequently, media of understanding must be used. The basic medium of understanding is language, but in the educational context it is e.g. concepts related to the children's world of experience.
- It is improbable that the child reacts in accordance with what the teacher says. Consequently, effect media must be used. These are techniques of persuasion, rhetoric etc. At a societal level it is the development of symbolically generalised communication media, i.e. media that are functionally adequate to a particular set of problems.

Summing up, the theory of educational media can be defined as one part of the general theory of media pedagogy. The theory of educational media includes firstly that particular form of communication that has developed as a result of the functional differentiation of upbringing and teaching with its special code, intentionality and application of specialised roles. Secondly it includes a specification and analysis of those media of dissemination, understanding and effect, which have emerged for educational communication, and the ways in which they are used.

If the general theory of the emergence of media as an answer to the improbabilities of communication is specified in relation to educational media, one should start by looking at the classroom as a system of interaction.

Also in this interaction system three media types can be identified:

First, the teacher must speak loud enough to be heard by the students. Also a particular asymmetry must be established allowing the teacher to talk freely, while the pupils must raise their hands in order to contribute. Finally, the physical and organisational classroom can be analysed as a dissemination medium. The students are organised so that they can see the teacher, but cannot necessarily see each other. The teacher stands on a raised platform with his desk and chair. He speaks, as tradition says, "ex cathedra". And he has monopolised the specialised teaching dissemination media: The blackboard, the overhead projector, the maps, etc. Thus, the particular physical and social design and organisation of the classroom is part of the dissemination aspect of educational media.

This can as well be found in e-learning systems. The most important point is that with e-learning the teacher can reach the students independently of time and place. Also, in learning management systems the roles are not equally distributed, but the teacher has certain "rights". However, one of the problems with e-learning is that the teacher cannot tell whether the students are connected or not.

Second, the teacher must do his best to make himself understood. He must use concepts that the pupils are expected to understand, and he must refer to examples from the children's world of experience and relevance. We all know that abstract decimal fractions are "translated" into pieces of layer cake, and that technical terms are coupled with terms from everyday life.

A basic characteristic of communication is that understanding must always be checked. "When one communicative action follows another, it tests whether the preceding communication was understood. (...) The test can turn out negative, and then it often provides an occasion for reflective communication about communication. But to make this possible (or to make it unnecessary) a test of understanding must always accompany, so that some part of attention is always detached to control understanding." (Luhmann 1995 p. 143 [1984]). We know this mechanism from the turn-taking theory. Communication is structured into turns, and it is important for the speaker through small signs of communicative acts to see that he is actually both heard and understood. In educational communication this is formalised into phases of question-answering, but also into systems of tests and examinations. Thus, tests and examinations are not, as reform pedagogy might have it, means of rigid control and suppression, but are ways to test that educational communication is successful.

Also, the aspect concerning media for understanding can be found in e-learning systems. The most obvious example is that educational concepts and themes are translated into concepts and themes closer to the experiential world of the pupils. The best-known case is Seymour Papert's classical "Turtle Talk" (cf. Papert 1980). Here, mathematics is translated into movements on the screen, and it is asserted that children understand moving images better than mathematical formula. Adding to that it is believed that they prefer anthropomorphised animals for abstract graphs, thus raising the level of relevance of the communication. Other examples are simulation systems, which of course are nothing else than translations from one medium into another. However, one should bear in mind that nothing can be translated from one medium of understanding into another without side effects. Meaning is bound to a particular context, and with e.g. "Turtle Talk" the risk is that children believe, it is about the life of turtles and not about universal mathematical principles.

One of the inherent problems of e-learning systems is to support the test-of-understanding aspect. Normally, understanding is tested by the application of secondary observation media. This can be done thanks to the physical presence of teachers and students in the classroom interaction. The teacher can observe the level of interest and/or absence of the students by observing their eye-contact, the nodding of their heads, and their small communicative expressions of being present. This is difficult to do in e-learning systems. The reason is that reflective communication of communication normally happens in supplementary observation media, which are often absent in digitally mediated interaction. One speaks to another person through the telephone, wondering whether he or she actively listens, or is busy doing sometimes else. In e-learning one misses the second, reflective medium of eye-contact, of the pupils nodding their heads etc. This is sometimes compensated for by the development of formalised test systems. However, the cost of doing so is that a signal of miss-trust is sent.

Third, the teacher must try to overcome the third improbability of communication, the creation of effect. Even when the students hear and understand what is being said, they do not necessarily follow the teacher. Here, effect media must be applied. The teacher aims to be appealing and convincing, i.e. to create an effect. He talks appealingly to the children, he uses a wide repertoire of rhetorical means, and he would – at least in earlier days – use sanctions or rewards in order to be successful.

According to Luhmann, the most important means in society of motivating acceptance is the emergence of symbolically generalised communication media, i.e. media that are functionally adequate to the particular problem addressed in the act of communication. This mechanism can be found in the functional specialisation of teaching. One lesson is about mathematics, another concerns literature, and it is obvious that this increases the motivation for acceptance, particularly, of course, if participation is based on free choice.

However, in an educational context the most important means to create effect is the physical presence in the classroom interaction. To make a promise – e.g. the promise of doing as one has been told – the physical proximity of the other is important. Therefore, rituals of promise often imply physical contact, including ritualisation of potential sanctions. I touch your shoulder with my sword, when you promise to support me as head of the club. In mafia contexts, offers that cannot be refused are followed by highly ritualised hugs and kisses.

Looking at e-learning, it is difficult to compensate for the physical presence and thus to create effects and motivate acceptance. Often, the reaction is to supplement e-learning with physical presence, that is to practice so-called blended learning. In this way one benefits from the strong potentials of e-learning, that it is an excellent dissemination medium, because it combines the bridging of physical distance with the personal contact, at the same time as compensating for the disadvantages of the e-learning medium, that it is difficult to use as an effect medium.

But of course e-learning systems aim at compensating for the weakness of the effect function, for instance by increasing its fascination potentials and by including mechanisms of reward and punishment. The most well-known mechanism is to use the genre of computer games for educational purposes. One can appeal to the engagement of the pupils, and one can include mechanisms of reward and punishment, which would otherwise not be accepted within a reform pedagogical context, because they belong to the game context.

Reflectivity

We have now identified the particularities of educational communication and of education as a medium for communication. We have also analysed the improbabilities of communication in general and of educational communication in particular, and we have specified the three basic medium-forms of educational communication: the dissemination-medium form, the understanding-medium form, and the effect-medium form.

However, it should also be emphasised that teaching – as communication in general – is reflective. All communication implies communication about communication, as Watzlawick once said (cf. Watzlawick et al. 1968). In educational contexts it is obvious that both students and teachers know that this is the case, and that they act in accordance with this fact.

Concerning the classroom interaction, Luhmann talks about "wahrnehmen des wahrgenommenwerdens" (Luhmann 2002 p. 105), that is the fact that the child perceives being perceived, that the pupil or the student is aware of being observed. We know it right from the early upbringing. The child puts on its best behaviour, when it is being observed by adults – or it might on the contrary make faces at the expectations of the educational view. We know it from the classroom interaction, where pupils can avoid being observed by looking into their papers, or where they can try to catch the eye of the teacher in order to catch his or her attention. The trick is to be observed at the right and not at the wrong moment. We know it when the pupils get home from school making ironic remarks about the teacher. "What did the teacher say about today's poem?" the interested parents might ask. When the child answers: "Blah, blah, blah", both parties know that the child – consciously or unconsciously – has practised the art of surviving tedious communication without letting others know that this is the case.[5]

But also the educator and the teacher know that this is the case. He or she knows that the pupil observes the observation of the teacher. They both know that teaching is a game, that is a performance in front of an audience, although the contract between actor and audience is different from the contract between teacher and pupil. The teacher acts. But in the classroom the audience should not be entertained, but educated.

Thus, teaching and education are characterised by double reflectivity, or by first and second order reflectivity. Both parties mutually observe the other's communication, and they observe that this observation is being observed. Consequently, educational media must be able to make this double reflectivity possible. That kind of distance education medium that makes this reflective observation impossible is not an appropriate medium. It must support the signal from the pupils that they know that they are being observed, and it must support the signal from the teacher that he knows that the pupils know and signal this.

---

5. Thanks to Yngve Nordkvelle for mentioning this example.

Communicative relations: Student-subject, student-teacher, teacher-subject

I have looked at education as mediated communication, at the use of media in education, and at the reflective potentials of educational media.

However, educational media are also influenced and formed by the fact that they mediate different communicative relations.

In pedagogy one often talks about the educational triangle between student, teacher and subject. There are three different communicative relations, one relation between the student and the subject, a second relation between the student and the teacher, and a third relation between the teacher and the subject. For each of these relations specific types of media can be specified.

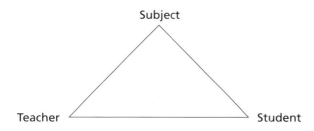

The relationship between student and subject is mediated by that type of media, which according to tradition are called "educational material" or "learning" means. In system theoretical terms educational materials, for instance textbooks, can be defined as a medium that makes operative coupling between science and education and structural coupling between subject and student possible. Let me use the textbook in mathematics as an example. First, it functions as a "book of translation" or a "book of transformation". It is based on scientific evidence, but it translates or transforms this evidence so that it can be understood and appreciated by the pupils. Second, it is a "book of intentionalisation". In principle it is only interested in scientific evidence in so far as this can be used for changing or developing the pupils into the intended direction, i.e. stimulate them to learn mathematics according to the curriculum plans.

In the era of electronic media, digital textbooks are supposed to support the same double operative and structural coupling. First of all scientific evidence is popularised through visualisation etc., and it is made relevant by being integrated into a narrative context. Second, it is intentionalised by being structured into bits and pieces that fit into the curriculum structure. Computer game based teaching material is an obvious example of this. The student can enter and explore a visualised world where he or she can solve problems, score points and reach the next game play level.

The relationship between student and teacher is mediated by that type of media, which according to tradition is called "instruction" or "teaching" material.[6] One might call these media "dramaturgic" media, because it is their function to support teaching as a specialised type of acting. In this sense the teacher's podium, blackboard, chalk, overhead projector, pointer etc. – "instruction materials" – should be called instruction or teaching media. Even the classroom in its physical layout is a medium – a stage – for teaching.

Only with new, digital media it has become possible to transform the classroom interaction – i.e. the mutual observation of persons being present – into a mediation of persons who are not physically present. With new, interactive dissemination media, students at one place can observe a teacher at another place, or students at one time can observe a teacher teaching at another time of the day. Of course, one of the challenges is to make interaction possible, that is to allow students and teachers to act in first and second order reflection modes (cf. above). Learning management systems are systems aimed at transforming classroom interaction into mediated interaction between persons who are separated in time and space. Actually, traditional textbooks can be defined as media for a teacher's interaction with a pupil, from whom he is separated in place and time. However, most often textbooks are designed in order not to replace teaching, but in order to support teaching.

Finally, the relationship between teacher and subject is mediated by that type of media which can support the teacher's management of

---

6. If one compare the English terms "education/teaching material" and "instruction material" it is obvious that the distinction isn't clear between the mediation of the student-subject relationship and the student-teacher relationship. It is clearer in Danish: "læremiddel" versus "undervisningsmiddel".

the subject. The most obvious example is the so-called "teacher's book". Here, the student's textbook is supplemented by a book for the teacher. This is a book with ideas and instructions for the teacher: How should he understand the scientifically based subject, how should he make the best use of the textbook, and how should he organise and stage his teaching? Also, this type of medium can give solutions to the textbook assignments, provide additional material and perspectives to the subject, or support the teacher with examples, pictures, suggested work forms etc. In some extreme cases the teacher's book is a teaching manual.

Of course, the "teacher's book" concept can also be found within the realm of digital media, often with instruction tools, CD-Rom or DVD materials, or with links to network-based digital resources. Also, however, the relationship between teacher and subject can be mediated more directly by providing the teacher with production means for his or her own production of teaching material.

Summing up this section, three types of educational media can be identified:

– Subject oriented media – textbooks etc. – for mediating the student-subject relationship.
– Teaching oriented media – teaching equipment – for mediating the teacher- student relationship.
– Subject production oriented media for mediating the teacher-subject relationship.

In addition to their individual qualities, all these three types of media are characterised by the intentionality, that they are aimed at changing individuals according to curricula. They are also characterised by being supposed to reduce the three improbabilities of educational communication: dissemination, understanding and effect.

Rules/self-organisation, Reality/virtuality

In addition to the above, I will make the assertion that education can be characterised in relation to two dimensions, both of which are relevant for the understanding of educational media. One dimension is the one between rules and self-organisation. The other is the one between reality and virtuality.

I would claim that the distinction between rules and self-organisation or between hetero- and self-organisation corresponds to the distinction between game and play. In the game, rules are pre-defined. One cannot change the rules for soccer or chess while the game is going on. In contrast, in the play the participants create – or at least negotiate and modify – the rules while the play is going on. One can play Indians and cowboys while negotiating and changing the rules for being dead and alive. "You have to hit me harder, in order to kill me". Or: "I have already been dead for ten minutes. Now I am allowed to join the play again."

All teaching can be placed on the scale between hetero- and self-organisation, i.e. between gaming and playing. Teaching is a game in so far as the rules are defined in advance, or in so far as the definition of rules are monopolised by the teacher. However, teaching can also look like play, for example because the pupils can appeal for the rules to be changed. "Shouldn't we just talk?" the pupils might ask, or: "Shouldn't we decide that the pupils are decision-makers today?"

All teaching can also be placed on the scale between reality and virtuality. Education in democracy is not necessarily democratic, and education concerning pollution does not pollute. Education is a game or a play, it is not reality. The reason why education is separated from reality is that reality is irreversible, while things can be repeated in another way or even reversed in education. Thus, education is necessarily "about" reality or "as if" reality, no matter how much reform pedagogy longs for reality. Luckily, soldiers have to read about war and to simulate war before going to war.

What has this to do with media? I think it is illustrative to look at the computer game as an educational medium. Let us imagine a multi-user game that simulates organisational communication, for example a game for pupils who are supposed to try how democratic communication functions. Or it might be a game for employees in an organisation, who are supposed to go through a number of organisational scenarios.

A multi-user computer game is a medium, which regulates the relationship between the actors and which stimulates the actors to reflect their mutual relations. In some cases the game rules are defined *ex ante*. Then the game is like football or chess. In other cases it is possible to negotiate and modify the rules during the game. Then it is rather like a role-play activity. Often, both things are possible. Then it can be called a "game-play".[7] No matter how the multi-user game has been constructed, it supports the reflection of the relationship between necessity and emergence, i.e. between hetero-organisation and self-organisation. By playing the game – or the play – one can observe oneself as a game-subject choosing between accepting the rules of the game or trying to change these rules.

In addition, the computer game – not least that special kind of computer game called "pervasive gaming" – is placed on the dimension between virtuality and reality. Pervasive gaming is a type of computer game, which does not happen in the virtual world, e.g. on the computer screen, but which happens in the real world. As an example one can play multi-user war-game by using a GPS-system and handheld computers. The basic effect of this is that the unbearable easiness of the game – that it is reversible, that is doesn't have consequences, but can be re-done – is being confronted by the irreversibility of reality, no matter whether this irreversibility is based in space or time. One cannot revert time or be present at more than one place.

One illustration is provided by a simple, early and successful example of pervasive gaming: Tamagotchi. The simple rule of the game is that the player is supposed to keep a physical avatar alive by feeding and stimulating him/her. If one doesn't manage to do so – for example because it has been forgotten or hasn't been stimulated in time – the Tamagotchi dies.[8]

In this way the computer game as educational medium illustrates the classical relationship between virtuality and reality in education. On the one hand it is, as already argued, necessary for education to be virtual. On the other hand this is the weakness of education: That it isn't "real" or "serious". With pervasive gaming the relationship between the aesthetics of education and the irreversible necessity of reality can be thematised.

---

7. Thanks to my colleague Bo Kampmann Walther for suggesting this play (game?) on words.
8. I have got the example from Espen Aarseth at the IT University in Copenhagen.

Media genres

Until now I have tried to present the dimensions of a theory of media education, media socialisation and educational media. In this final section of the chapter I would like to present the subject from the point of view of a number of specific media genres: Children's films, museums, playgrounds, and computer games.

A children's film exemplifies the basic dilemma: Is it – like children's books – an educational media genre or is it an art media genre? On the one hand, children's films are often made with a pedagogical or didactical goal. Like educational communication in general, they are supposed to support the realisation of a specific educational objective. On the other hand, children's films and books have the same function as any other work of art: to make an aesthetic judgment – a judgment of taste, which by definition is highly subjective[9] – socially communicative (Baecker 2005 p. 17). The function of art is to make "...perception ("Wahrnehmung") available for communication..." as Luhmann says (Luhmann 2000a p. 48 [1985 p. 82]).

One thing is obvious. That children's film as media genre is placed between two differentiated functional systems in society: Education and art. This is not a question of an "ontological" dilemma. This is not an inherent tension in the children's film as such, and it is also not the case that the film will be of less value if it has a pedagogical objective, or that it becomes of high value or "dangerous" for a child audience, if it has an artistic objective. Rather, the point is that the same phenomenon appears differently depending on the observational position: Is it observed from the point of view of the system of art or of the educational system?

Museums, playgrounds, computer games as well can be observed from different viewpoints. Museums have a scientific function, and they have a life-world function, i.e. to make the past observable. However, they also have an educational function: Museums are educational media.

Something similar can be said about playgrounds. On the one

---

9. Cf. Niklas Luhmann's observation that "...the notion of taste aims at the necessity of a (...) selection without being able to provide a criterion". Luhmann 2000a p. 381 (footnote 86), [Luhmann 1985 p. 387].

hand children are supposed to develop themselves freely and without any hidden concerns. On the other hand that are also supposed to learn something, e.g. to control their bodies. The same dilemma can be identified with computer games. Like films and books they are aimed at aesthetic realisation, but at the same time they have a pedagogical function: They are supposed to educate. Consequently, all these media can be observed through the optics of media pedagogy, i.e. as educational media. Let me by means of a final example suggest, what could be said about the playground as educational medium based on this approach and with the above considerations in mind.

First of all, the playground incarnates a specific consideration of purpose. Its clear colours, its potentials for free activities, its organic forms etc. – all this is designed from considerations concerning what is beneficial for the bodily activities of children. It incarnates a pedagogical ideal and an educational teleology.

The function of the playground as a dissemination medium, a medium of understanding and an effect medium is subtle. There isn't any explicit or specific message, which must be mediated. Still, however, it is obvious that a certain teleology is supposed to be realised. The playground is supposed to attract children with its tempting visibility. It is supposed to "translate" a pedagogical message. And it is supposed to have an effect, namely to stimulate children to be cheerful, bodily strong, trustful and expressive. In addition, many modern playgrounds should stimulate collective activities. Yes, playgrounds are strong effect media.

Should playgrounds stimulate reflection? I suppose not. Playgrounds are supposed to stimulate spontaneity. The children are not supposed to be able to observe that they are being observed, for instance by being contextualised into a pedagogical framework. Supposedly, this is due to an evolution theoretical consideration: Reflection is believed to occur later in the child's individual evolution history.

However, it is quite obvious that playgrounds are placed in the spectrum between freedom and necessity, and between virtuality and reality. That they are placed in the spectrum between freedom and necessity can be seen from the fact that playgrounds are designed in the interval between free activity – play – and rule-based activity, game. One can use a climbing frame or a swing for many things, but not for everything.

Basically, however, playgrounds as educational media are placed in the interval between virtuality and reality. They pay tribute to the principle of so-called experience-based pedagogy. Life – not even early child life – is uncommitted easiness. It is sounder to be at the playground than to sit in front of the television set, is the implicit message of the playground (and its pedagogical designers). Of course, the playthings and climbing frames must be certificated according to safety regulations. However, the basic point is that if one hurts oneself, when one falls off the swing, this fulfils an educational purpose.

Conclusion

The intention of the present chapter has been to present the overall structure of media pedagogy.

Media pedagogy includes three basic elements: First, it includes a theory of media education, i.e. a theory of the way in which one can teach the pupils and students to use media, and how one can teach them about media as a phenomenon in society. Second, it includes a theory of education within the context of "media-socialisation", i.e. within the context that mass media represent a special aspect of socialisation in relation to the pupils. Third, it includes a theory of educational media.

This latter part includes the identification and analysis of the following aspects: First, it includes the fact that education represents a particular form of communication that has developed as a result of the functional differentiation of upbringing and teaching. Thus, education is a symbolically generalised medium with its special code, intentionality and application of specialised roles. A theory of educational media must specify this particular form of symbolically generalised medium. Second, it includes the fact that in order to make educational communication at least a bit less improbable, specialised media of dissemination, understanding and effect have emerged. A theory of educational media must specify the particularities of these media forms. Third, it includes the importance of supporting both first order and second order observations in the classroom interaction. Fourth, it includes a specification of three classroom interaction relations: Student-teacher, student-subject and teacher-subject, and it includes a specification of the specific media forms developed for mediating these relations. Fifth, it includes the basic distinctions of hetero-organisation/self-organisation and of virtuality/reality in educational communication, and it includes analyses of the ways in which educational media can make these distinctions observable.

Of course, a theory of media pedagogy and of educational media includes the forms, applications and usages of digital media for education, and the specific aim of the present chapter was to present a framework for a theory of digital educational media. However, I have tried to demonstrate that theories of digital educational media, e.g. e-learning, must be based on a general media pedagogical theory, for instance the theory that has been outlined in this chapter. In the next chapter I will turn specifically to the theory of e-learning.

4. E-Learning

– A Knowledge Theoretical Approach

Introduction

In the field of e-learning, i.e. the use of information and communication technologies in education, there is a stark contrast between high policy expectations and a lack of theoretical clarity. The resulting paradox is that a lot is *done* within the field of e-learning, but very little is *known*. European e-learning plans are introduced and e-learning activities at national and institutional levels are initiated. These activities are measured in terms of cost-ratio and evaluation schemes. But we often don't know what is measured or according to which criteria evaluation studies are performed because there is a lack of theoretical enlightenment concerning e-learning.

The underlying problem is not that e-learning theories do not exist or that e-learning research programmes have not been supported, but that many incompatible paradigms are at play. One paradigm is used by proponents of e-learning, while others are used by critics. Even worse, these incompatible theoretical positions are not as a rule explained. This results in a state of double contingency. One part supports e-learning based on his or her hidden reasons. Another part is against, but based on quite another form of reasoning. For me, the problem is not that we cannot judge whether e-learning *per se* is good or bad. This would be an impossible task. The important question is 'how' e-learning is judged to be good or bad, i.e. according to which criteria this is said to be the case.

Confronted with this situation, the first step must be to actually specify what lies behind the current e-learning debate: what are the hidden criteria? The next step is to elaborate a common framework for discussion. In the present chapter my suggested contribution for such a framework is a knowledge theoretical communication paradigm.

Thus, in this chapter I first identify and explicate four dominant, but normally non-articulated and mutually incompatible paradigms in the current e-learning debate. Secondly, I suggest that e-learning should be seen in a communication theoretical perspective, assuming that education is a specialised form of communication aimed at changing people in accordance with politically defined goals, using oral, print or digital media for this communication. This implies that computers and digital networks are seen as media of communication.

However, in order to further qualifying the communication paradigm I suggest that we specify educational communication as knowledge-stimulating communication. The advantage of this approach is that based on a knowledge classification scheme, the impact of different types of computer-mediated communication in e-learning for education can be specified: E-learning is not *per se* good or bad, but different forms of e-learning support different types of knowledge-acquisition.

Current E-Learning Paradigms

As already stated, expectations concerning e-learning, i.e. the use of information and communication technologies (ICTs) for the support of learning processes, is high, and it is generally assumed that the use of ICT will increase the efficiency of training and education activities, both in formalised learning institutions and in the lifelong education of the general population.

This, however, contrasts strongly with the lack of theoretical clarity regarding the understanding of e-learning. This should come as no surprise, though. E-learning is a new phenomenon, and no consensus regarding the theoretical basis for observing e-learning has yet been reached. Even the definitions and designations are numerous. The European Commission has suggested the following definition in connection with its so-called e-learning programme for 2004-2006: E-learning includes "...the use of new multimedia technologies and the Internet to improve the quality of learning by facilitating access to resources and services as well as remote exchanges and collaboration." In itself, this is indeed an extremely broad definition. However, the situation is actually worse. Over the course of just a few years, e-learning has been referred to in Europe as distance teaching, technology-supported teaching, flexible learning, computer-based learning and network-based learning. As we shall see, these names contain intended or unintended references to the various theoretical approaches to e-learning which have been around.

The problem with this lack of definitional and theoretical clarity is that the basis is unclear when one discusses e-learning and the expected effects of e-learning. It is often difficult to see what is meant by the concept in one example or the other and to know which forms of e-learning are being referred to when expectations of effects are presented.

The lack of clarity is, among other reasons, due to the fact that the approaches to e-learning are based on theoretical positions which are often not made explicit. It is therefore important to identify the theoretical foundations of the various e-learning strategies. I believe one can distinguish between at least four paradigms, with corresponding notions of how to construct e-learning systems: the instructivist paradigm, the body-phenomenological paradigm, the activity-theoretical paradigm and the constructivist paradigm.

The Instructivist Paradigm

The paradigm which dominated the understanding of e-learning from its beginning until virtually the end of the 20th century was the so-called instructivist paradigm, which typically has behaviourist roots. In this paradigm, learning is conceived of as a causal result of teaching or other forms of external influence. E-learning systems based on this position will therefore emphasise and support the possibilities of instructor-led teaching. One would hardly speak of an 'instructivist view of learning', because learning represents an activity engaged in by pupils or students. Rather, one would speak of an instructivist view of *teaching.* E-learning systems based on this position typically support instructor-centred communication, lectures, distribution of materials and possibly aptitude tests.

The instructivist paradigm was closely related to an understanding of ICT as an instrument for transporting or processing data.

From the outset, i.e. from the 1960s, the understanding of e-learning was based on an entirely traditional conception of tools or technologies, where the computer was conceived of as a tool or a machine for transporting and processing the raw material of the machine: data. Understanding was taken over from the prothetic technologies, i.e. those technologies whose function is predicated on a physical influence of physical matter. The shovel or the mechanical digger function because they move earth. The lorry or the train transports raw material from one place to another. The centrifuge, the mixer or the chemical plant mixes raw materials, thereby creating new materials.

If new educational technologies were conceptualised as transport technologies, one would speak of ICT-supported learning as 'distance learning'. In the United States in particular, large-scale programmes were instituted where lectures were disseminated through the medium of television. This later became the Internet, which functioned as the main transport opportunity. The attractiveness of the new technology was that it allowed for the almost infinite dissemination of data. The idea was that data could be moved around the world.

If, however, emphasis were placed on the computer as a machine for processing data, one would focus on "programmed teaching", i.e. factual learning as the effect of repetition. The resulting view was that a computer was valid as an educational technology because it was both more patient and more capable of variations than any teacher and could therefore adapt to the level and standpoint of the individual student on the basis of multiple-choice tests. As already mentioned, this approach was based on a mechanical input-output paradigm: After having been affected by the computer as an input device, the student will answer the question, i.e. producing an output. Depending on the answer, the computer then prepares the next stimulus. The process can continue without any limitations, i.e. until the student provides a satisfactory answer and the computer can proceed to the next theme.

In both cases the dominant teaching theoretical perspective was behaviourist. The machine metaphor was applied to the computer, which was seen as an 'artificial intelligence'. But the machine metaphor was also applied to human intelligence, which was seen as an advanced computational device. Based on this, it was obvious to assume that there was a causal relationship between teaching input and learning outcome: The more people data could be disseminated to, the more people learned something. The better the machine was in varying the data relative to feedback from learners, the higher the yield.

The Body-Phenomenological Paradigm

The instructivist paradigm already came under strong criticism in the 1970s, and during the 1980s and 1990s this critique developed into its own paradigm. The basic critical assumption was that there is no reason to believe that learning can be understood as a simple input/output phenomenon. It is more appropriate to consider the pupil or student as a non-trivial system characterised by a given input not resulting in a corresponding output. From here a number of theoretical positions developed, which are far from mutual agreement, and each of which has its specific implications for the understanding of learning and e-learning.

The paradigm that developed as a kind of opposition to instructivism is what one might term the body-phenomenological paradigm. It has its roots in modern phenomenology, with Martin Heidegger as the general reference source (cf. Heidegger 1986 [1927]), and with the French phenomenologist Maurice Merleau-Ponty (1945) as the specific inspiration to understanding the role of the body in psychological and intellectual activities. In relation to digital communication and e-learning, this has been picked up upon particularly by Hubert L. Dreyfus (cf. Dreyfus 2001). The emphasis here is on the bodily dimension of teaching and learning: We do not learn with our intellect alone, but also by virtue of bodily presence. Not least, according to this view, advanced forms of learning are supported by our physical presence in the teaching situation, partly because an intensity is created which digitally mediated communication does not provide, and partly because the body and bodily emotions are important in imparting meaning to things. On the basis of this position one would therefore recommend that only very simple and routine forms of teaching should take place through e-learning systems, while more advanced forms of teaching should be delivered by face-to-face communication.

In relation to this, the view of computers and the Internet as technologies came to be replaced by a theory according to which computers and the Internet can be understood as media or symbol machines, i.e. so-called non-prothetic tools. According to this, the computer is defined as a device analogous to the clock, which does not work by virtue of its physical influence on a raw material, but by symbolising a phenomenon, e.g. time. The clock and the computer are symbolic media. In extension of this, the computer and the digital network are seen as a complex mediated system through which a programmer communicates with a large number of users via a programme. The Internet in particular is considered a networked medium of communication with unlimited possibilities of feedback.

Many of the pedagogical paradigms in the above-mentioned list attached themselves to this view of technology, among them the phenomenological paradigm. The argument for the significance of the body in a teaching and learning context goes as follows: We do not understand only with our intellect. No, 'Our body plays a crucial role in our being able to make sense of things so as to see what is relevant, our ability to make things matter to us and so to acquire skills, our sense of the reality of things, our trust in other people, and finally, our capacity for making the unconditional commitments that give meaning to our lives.' So writes Hubert Dreyfus (Dreyfus 2001, p. 90) in explicit extension of this.

The critical conclusion, which Dreyfus draws himself, is that the Internet can be useful in teaching, when it comes to accessing facts and for routine exercises, i.e. for the acquisition of what I call first order knowledge (cf. chapter 1). When it comes to improvisation, situated behaviour or what Dreyfus calls the 'expert level', physical presence is necessary. According to Dreyfus, only in a classroom setting, where the teacher and the learner feel they are running a risk in each other's presence and can both expect criticism, are those conditions present which further the development of competent routine and one can only become an expert by acting in the real world. (Dreyfus 2001)

There are two types of objections to this. One is that *all* teaching is mediated and, more generally, that all human collective activity is conditioned by media. There is no such thing as a pre-mediated, 'authentic' presence or being together. When we interact in a classroom we do it through a physical medium – sound waves in the air – and a symbolic medium, i.e. language. When we read books we engage in a thoroughly mediated activity. One cannot distinguish absolutely between embodied and non-embodied presence, but one has to distinguish between *different* types of mediation. Obviously, however, the media spectrum is broader in the classroom than on the Internet.

The second type of objection is media optimistic. It makes the claim that interaction and communication is about bandwidth and that human perception uses a certain, but not unlimited bandwidth. According to the Danish research journalist Tor Nørretranders, this is 11 megabits per second. '11 Mbps is all we need and all we can use. 11 Mbps is the bandwidth of human sensory experience.' (Nørretranders 1997, p. 151, my translation) So it is only a question of time before the Internet can completely substitute physical presence.

Between these two positions there is the characteristic middle position, which advocates 'blended learning'. Some teaching activities – the acquisition of facts in particular, according to Dreyfus – can take place on the Internet and at the computer, while others should take place in a physical group. The teaching challenge consists in combining the different types of teaching in an appropriate way, i.e. to create the correct level of 'blended learning'.

The Activity-Theory Paradigm

A third paradigm which has influenced the understanding of e-learning is the activity theory paradigm, which often refers to Lev Vygotsky's work (Vygotsky 1962 and 1978) and which is at times also described as 'constructionist'. This position is, among others, very widespread in the Nordic countries. The basic idea is that learning is a result of the individual and collective activity of students, and concepts such as 'collaborative learning' and 'communities of practice' are widely used. According to this view, learning takes place by virtue of learning-oriented constructive work. Systems based on this position therefore emphasise the provision of facilities to support group work, chatting, etc., i.e. facilities for collaboration, exchange of experiences, knowledge sharing etc.

Within the activity-theoretical paradigm, e-learning can be described and classified from the various network morphologies that are formed: Do these networks support collaboration and collective practices, or do they not? This position can be found in the Danish Ministry of Science's 2003 report on e-learning, where four models are proposed:

- E-learning where the learners never physically meet, but only learn through the computer, and where there is no dialogue among those involved.
- E-learning where the learners never physically meet, but where dialogue between the participants is supported in virtual environments.
- E-learning where the learners alternate between learning in a classroom or other form of physical interaction and working independently with their computer, e.g. at home.
- E-learning where the learners only learn by being physically together, e.g. a class, and where the computer is used as a tool in teaching. (Ministry of Science, Technology and Innovation 2003, p. 6-13)

In addition to a morphological classification as the one suggested by the Danish Ministry of Science, both sceptical and optimistic activity theoretical positions are found. Some emphasise that teaching is best done as an interaction between physically present persons. If that is the case, the use of computers or Internet-based communication would be ill-advised. Others assert that it is the use of computers and the Internet, which can extend the possibilities of interaction, so that they are not only found in the physical classroom or the group of people present, but can be created everywhere, that is to say as so-called 'virtual classrooms'.

The Constructivist Paradigm

Finally, one ought also to mention the constructivist paradigm, which has many different references, but which, among other sources, is based on Niklas Luhmann and Karl-Eberhard Schorr's works on pedagogy and the education system (cf. e.g. Luhmann and Schorr 1982 and Luhmann 2002). The fundamental view here is that education is a structural coupling between two different activities, i.e. teaching and learning. Teaching is seen as a specialised form of communication, while learning is seen as an individual or group-based activity where knowledge is constructed. The basic challenge of education is to overcome the problem that there is no direct input-output relation between teachers and students, i.e. no transportation of knowledge from one to the other. Students can only observe the mediated communication selections made by the teacher and by other students and, based on these and on supplementary observations, the student must construct his or her own understanding. Learning in the classroom as an interaction system takes place as structural couplings between the students in the classroom and the communication orchestrated by the teacher.

Seen from this position, e-learning systems must both support teaching communication, primarily the students' observations of the teacher (traditionally through oral and print media, now also through digital media), and the individual and collective learning processes, i.e. the self-referential processes of the learning system, and it should first and foremost support appropriate structural couplings between the two activities such as one finds, for instance, in the specialised interaction system of the classroom (cf. Luhmann 2002).

From the constructivist paradigm one would focus on three basic elements: 1) how to meet the demand of supporting teaching communication, i.e. to make communicational selections observable by students, 2) how to comply with the requirement for reflections of the learners, and 3) how to support the student managing his or her competence development.

As regards at least points 1 and 2, the different types of conference-functions accompanying many e-learning systems will be useful: asynchronous conferences have the great quality of formalising dialogues in order to facilitate reflection and to make knowledge explicit, while the synchronous conferences have the quality of being a forum for spontaneous dialogues and therefore a great context for the elaboration of ideas between students.

As a particular interface for the interaction between the individual student and the teacher, among students, but also between the individual student and the education system one could mention the digital portfolio (cf. the last section of this chapter). Etymologically speaking, a portfolio is a briefcase for carrying personal papers. This is where one keeps one's curriculum vitae, official documents, but also personal notes.

The digital portfolio often contains a private working space and a public working space. In the public working space a differentiation can be made between spaces to which different users have access, for instance between a space, to which other students have access, and one to which the teacher has access. Thus, in a constructivist context the digital portfolio supports both teacher-student communication and individual and collective learning reflections of the students.

Another aspect that is interesting – especially in reference to the point number 3 – is that the student can place all his/her work (materials, notes, assignments, documents, recordings etc.) in a private working space to which, in principle, nobody else has access. This makes it possible to observe ones own learning, because the student regularly has to add new material to already existing material.

A Knowledge Theory of E-Learning

The Computer as Medium

In the 20th century the development of the prothetic technologies of industrial society reached its zenith in an almost complete automatisation of physical work processes.

At the same time, the 20th century was the time when the development of non-prothetic or symbolic technologies, i.e. technologies that support knowledge production, knowledge circulation and boundary crossing processes, was initiated. The theoretical foundation for the digital computer, i.e. for the universal symbol machine, was presented by Alan Turing in 1936. At around the same time, in 1948, Claude Shannon and Warren Weaver presented the first theory of digital communication, a theory based on a 1938 technical article by Shannon: 'A Symbolic Analysis of Relay and Switching Circuits'. The point is that this created the basis for non-physical machines, i.e. machines whose mode of functioning is independent of their physical basis. The universal computer is a computer, which is independent of a specific medium. It is a multimedia device in the true sense of the word.

This implies that the computer should be conceptualised as a communication medium, not only in the sense that the computer is the basic node in digital communication networks, but in the broader sense that the computer is a symbolic device, a device for the production, processing and dissemination of symbols. Because the functioning of computers is independent of their physical basis, computers are different from other communication media in the sense that they are not restricted by their physical form.

Books, newspapers, blackboards, television sets, video recorders, lecture halls, classrooms are media that are at least partly determined by their physical shape. One cannot do everything with a newspaper or in a lecture hall. One is restricted by the physical shape of the medium. However, a computer is different, because it can imitate any other medium. One can create digital books, blackboards or videos, and virtual classrooms, lecture halls or universities, i.e. imitate books, blackboards, videos, classrooms, lecture halls and universities.

In a limited period of ecstasy it was believed that this implied that digital books or virtual classrooms were identical to printed books and physical classrooms. This is indeed not the case: They are *imitations* of the book and the classroom. They are *mediatisations* of books and classrooms.

Teaching as stimulation of knowledge acquisition

Furthermore, as it has already been noticed, teaching can be defined as a specialised form of communication, i.e. the form of communication aimed at changing persons in accordance with predefined goals. The specific goals are defined in the curricula. However, the general goal is to stimulate pupils' and students' knowledge acquisition. Consequently, teaching can be defined as that specialised type of communication that is aimed at the stimulation of knowledge acquisition.

In accordance with these definitions I will present a knowledge theory of e-learning based on the categories of knowledge, learning and teaching presented in chapters 1 and 2. This approach builds on and further develops the above-mentioned constructivist approach to teaching as communication. The simple idea is that teaching is specialised communication, which must always involve one or more media. Any communication is mediated. With the computer – standalone computers and computers linked into digital networks – as a universal medium, i.e. a device that can imitate any other medium, new potentials have emerged for supporting educational communication. The pupil or the student can observe his or her environment – the teacher or lecturer, the other pupils or students, the teaching material – through new dissemination and symbolic media. This may influence the classroom as a complex and delicate interaction system, in which students observe the teacher's communication selections and order to construct understanding, in which students observe each other and in which the teacher observes the students' communicative selections as a direct or indirect sign of their acquisition of knowledge. This may influence the student-to-student interactions, and it may influence the individual activities of the students.

However, as all these activities are aimed at the stimulation of knowledge acquisition, I will build on the theory and categorisation of knowledge presented in chapters 1 and 2. This, then, is the foundation of my knowledge theoretical communication paradigm for e-learning.

Knowledge Theory

What is knowledge? According to the theory proposed in chapter one in this book, knowledge is a concept to describe the way in which a meaning-based system (e.g. a psychic system – a student in the classroom – or an organisation) handles complexity in the surrounding world. Knowledge is a source for transforming insecurity into security, but it is also – and increasingly so – a source for giving shape to insecurity, i.e. maintaining insecurity as insecurity but making it manageable, e.g. by having the ability to identify news, changes etc. and devising strategies to deal with them. In professional jargon, the first form of knowledge is called qualification, the other is called competence. So, knowledge is not a 'store' or an 'essence' but a relationship between internal complexity and complexity in the external world. In a collective organism, internal complexity is created by what Stuart Kauffman calls an autonomous agent, which can be a cell, a plant, an animal or a habitat, i.e. a biological system that takes care of handling relations with the surrounding world (cf. Kauffman, 2000). In a psychological system it can be the memory about categorisation of phenomena or about adequate strategies in certain situations. In an organisation it can be procedures, divisions of labour etc. Such knowledge can be externalised in the form of tools, machines and technologies. A crucial characteristic of knowledge is the fact that it is dynamic, i.e. its interaction with the surrounding world can lead to new knowledge. This is called learning, which is both an individual and organisational process.

Abilities: Skills and knowledge

In a modern society based on print media there is a tendency to confuse abilities with knowledge. One thinks that what we *can do* is identical with what we *know*. The natural scientist and theorist of knowledge, Michael Polanyi, in his groundbreaking 1966 book *The Tacit Dimension*, punctured this misapprehension. Besides what we know there is a 'tacit' dimension, that is to say all the things we can do, although we are not able to account for them. Beside our explicit knowledge – or rather: logically and historically prior to the explicit knowledge – there is tacit knowing.

This insight brings me to a fundamental distinction in the theory of knowledge: The sum total of human abilities can be split into skills and knowledge. Skills may be defined as immediate abilities, knowledge as reflected abilities (cf. chapter one in this book on the definition and categorisation of knowledge).

Let me provide an example. Learning to cycle is to acquire a skill. Any parent who has taught their children to cycle knows that it leads nowhere to go over the theory of cycling and then let the child apply the theory in practice. No, one has to fit a broomstick behind the saddle in order to help the child acquire the skill of cycling. Similarly, being able to cycle does not mean that one can account for how we do it.

This type of knowledge is not a knowledge that we 'have' but a knowledge that we practice or 'do'. Consequently, Polanyi does not speak about 'tacit knowledge' but about 'tacit knowing'. It is the processive nature of tacit knowing, which makes me designate it as a 'skill'.

From this Polanyi concludes that tacit knowing precedes explicit knowledge, i.e. skills precede knowledge. First we 'can do', then we 'know'.

This, however, does not, as some seem to believe, mean that 'skills' or 'tacit knowing' are especially deep or authentic. They are merely one side of the distinction between skills and knowledge, which make up the concept of ability. In modern society an increasing number of activities are knowledge-based. The very fact that we have to go to school to acquire formal or reflective abilities demonstrates that in modern society it is not sufficient to imitate the skills of one's parents and immediate surroundings. The differentiation of education into a functionally specialised, autopoietic educational system is therefore the institutional expression of the fundamental division of abilities into skills and knowledge.

But this, on the other hand, means that knowledge – reflective abilities – does not exist without skills, i.e. immediate abilities. Among other things, this has implications for the theory of learning. If learning something means to develop knowledge about something, this knowledge cannot exist or be generated without its twin: the skill, the immediate ability.

Concerning teaching and learning this means that there are limitations, not only to e-learning but to any kind of mediated teaching – and as already said any kind of formal teaching is mediated. Important things cannot be taught in so far as teaching means communication. They must be practised. On the other hand, other things can not be learned by doing, but only by communicating, i.e. as the result of formalised teaching. The difference is not, as Dreyfus believes, between simple and complex types of knowledge, but between skills and (explicit) knowledge.

Forms of knowledge – a systematic

As already argued and presented in chapter one, above, based on this definition of knowledge, four knowledge categories can be identified:

- 1st order knowledge: Object knowledge.
- 2nd order knowledge: Recursive knowledge, or situative knowledge.
- 3rd order knowledge: Reflective knowledge, or creative knowledge.
- 4th order knowledge: World knowledge.

Where the first three forms of knowledge represent observation-based forms of knowledge, i.e. relations between subject and world (including the subject's knowledge of itself as a subject in the world), the fourth form of knowledge is not knowledge about the world but the world as knowledge.

In the rest of this chapter I will apply these knowledge categories to the analysis of e-learning and to the differentiation of types of e-learning.

Knowledge technological forms of media

If one defines the computer as a medium rather than a machine, in accordance with the knowledge categories elaborated above one can identify four knowledge technological forms of media, because conceiving of the computer as a medium means considering the totality of the computer as a symbol-producing and symbol-communicating medium:

1. The computer as representation and simulation medium (1st order knowledge medium). Here, the computer functions as a medium that represents phenomena in the world, be it as simple references to facts, as interactive multimedia simulations of dynamic world phenomena or as representation of communication selections of the teacher.
2. The computer as a feedback medium (2nd order knowledge medium). Here, in classical terms the computer delivers a programmed feedback to the student's input. With the computer as medium the student can observe the effects in old and new contexts of what he or she already knows. His or her knowledge is 'reflected' back into the student by the computer.
3. The computer as interaction medium (3rd order knowledge medium). Here the computer system can function as a medium, for instance, for teaching as classroom interaction, both between student and teacher and between students. This approach makes it possible to support and/or to mimic the very complex communication processes in the classroom, i.e. the teacher's communicative stimulation of learning processes, the student's observation of the teacher's communicative selections and of the behaviour of other students, and the teacher's observation of student behaviour as an indirect expression of their comprehension. These processes can be mimicked regardless of whether the classroom is a physical space, i.e. independently of whether the parties to the interaction are physically present for each other. More importantly, however, the classroom is simulated as an arena of knowledge, i.e. as a community that has agreed upon certain paradigms or basic assumptions.
4. The total computer system (e.g. the Internet or an educational institution's Learning Management System) as a representation or simulation of world knowledge (4th order knowledge medium).

Here the computer is used to simulate phenomena in the external world, among them – by virtue of the computer's feedback potential – as a medium to simulate phenomena in the external world where the learner is an acting subject him/herself. Particularly, the Internet, or the World Wide Web, is a dissemination medium with a structure that combines global accessibility with self-generated addressability. This means that it functions as a semi-autopoietic knowledge system, i.e. as a structural simulation of the dynamic and self-developing system of world knowledge.

The computer as simulation medium: Social simulation

As long as knowledge technology is conceived of as a simple observational medium or as a mechanical stimulus/response medium, one is at the level of first order knowledge. The computer and the digital network can make knowledge accessible for observation and it can stimulate the cognitive processing of facts.

Only when one conceives of knowledge technology as a feedback and an interaction medium, one moves to second and third order knowledge, not least because knowledge technology provides a very effective simulation of the phenomenon that the 'I' is itself a subject endowed with agency in the world that is being simulated, and conversely that the 'I' is always already integrated into this world, that is to say that it is a mundanised subject.

This connection can be made intelligible in the following example, where I use the example of the computer as a social simulation medium. The example must be sketched out first, though.

My case study is one among many products from the Danish e-learning company Zenaria. It is a training system for a Danish bank's in-service training of staff involved in credit business. The system is based on interactive video and multiple choices. One follows simulated situations such as where a young couple approach the bank's credit adviser in order to apply for a loan for their newly opened bar. They require 10,000 euros for a music system, which in their view is a precondition for the bar to achieve its essential customer base.

In the interactive video the user acts the role of the acting subject, the credit adviser. After each line from the couple applying for the loan, the user has to choose from four possible responses and, depending on the response chosen, the dialogue continues. In other words, the conversation is split into turns, and in each turn the user has to place him/herself in the position of the credit adviser.

When a credit advice sequence is concluded, one can follow the customers home, where they comment on the advice given. Comments from the credit adviser's colleagues can be heard or one can see the credit adviser's psychological profile as expressed by the answers given.

This form of teaching through interactive, social simulation contains learning potential in relation to all of the four levels described above.

Firstly, factual knowledge is transmitted. The user sees how credit advice takes place. One is presented with the guidelines, according to which one has to operate in the bank in question. Factual observations are made.

Secondly, situational knowledge is transmitted. This is where the main emphasis lies. The user is placed in the position of the credit adviser and has to respond to an inquiry within short but realistic timeframes, i.e. handle a situation with its situationally based but unpredictable developmental path.

But the system also provides an opportunity for third order observation. One does not act only in an I/you relationship, but one also observes this I/you relationship from the outside, i.e. one observes ones own 'I' as an element in the relationship between ego and alter. This happens implicitly in the use of the video itself, as it constantly gives cause to self-observation ('what should I do in this situation?' 'which of the four answers is the most appropriate choice?' 'what would I do, if I were in their position?'), but it also happens explicitly, because one can observe the other party's reactions to the interaction and one is thereby forced to observe oneself through the eyes of the other, as happens through the comments of colleagues and in the psychological profile drawn up as a result of participation in this simulated social interaction.

Finally, one might claim that interactive simulation constitutes a fourth order knowledge system in itself. This means that the user's observation of the system of simulation itself is a world observation, but with the proviso that one is not observing a world but a simulation of a world. In reality, one is observing a second party's observation of the world one has to believe in, identify with and interact in. The other party can either be the bank's self-presentation through the producer, Zenaria, or it can be Zenaria and the premises of simulation, upon which Zenaria bases its productions.

Knowledge levels	Knowledge technological forms of knowledge: The computer as a simulation medium
First order knowledge	Factual knowledge: – Factual knowledge is made accessible to immediate observation
Second order knowledge	Recursive / situational knowledge: – Visuality (spatial recognisability) – Narrativity (temporal recognisability) – Interactivity (the I/you relationship)
Third order knowledge	Reflective / systemic knowledge: – Possibility of system observation: 'the I/you relationship' observed from the outside – Possibility of system transformation: simulated relearning.
Fourth order knowledge	Metaflective knowledge: – Possibility of context observation. – Possibility of observation of organisational and cultural conditions for knowledge forms 1-3

To sum up, one might say that e-learning systems such as the one analysed do not only make factual knowledge accessible to immediate observation, but the medium also makes situational recognisability possible. As a user one can recognise the situation one acts in, and one can in particular develop interactive competence in the you-I relationship. It makes systemic observation possible, because one can observe one's own interaction with the other from the outside, i.e. as an acting element in a system-embedded you-I relationship. It also makes possible a metasystemic reflection, because the medium provides possibilities for observing one's own situational and systemic being from the outside, i.e. from the position, which the organisational and cultural conditions for situational and systemic practice constitute. It is not least in this sense that the new usages of the computer as a knowledge-industrial medium constitute an interesting addition to the possibilities inherent in traditional media of education.

The computer as interaction medium: Digital portfolio

There has been significant development in recent years with regard to the application of computers as media for classroom interaction. Thus a number of experiments have been conducted using portable computers to support class interaction, both in the physical classroom as well as in the 'virtual' class, i.e. between teacher and students or between students outside the classroom and after school hours (cf. Mathiasen 2002).

At this point I would like to mention the so-called digital portfolio as a particular interface for the interaction between the individual student and the teacher and for the interaction among students. Etymologically speaking, a portfolio is a briefcase for carrying personal papers. This is where one keeps one's curriculum vitae, official documents, but also personal notes.

The basic structure of a digital portfolio is such that the student can access a server through the interface. The server contains the student's private working space (the portfolio) and a public working space. In the public working space a differentiation can be made between whether one is working in a space to which other students have access or one to which the teacher has access.

The basic point of the digital portfolio is that the student can place all his/her work (materials, notes, assignments, documents, recordings etc.) in a private working space to which, in principle, nobody else has access. This does not only provide unique multimedia work facilities, where e.g. digital video recordings can be combined with notes, sound recordings, scanned and downloaded materials etc., it also makes it possible to observe one's own learning, because the student regularly has to add new material to already existing material. If learning is defined as the process through which a system – in this case a psychological system, but it can also be an organisational system – stimulated by external influences changes its present way of functioning on the basis of its own preconditions and with a view to maintaining its present way of reacting (this is where it differs from 'socialisation', which is change stimulated by external influences with no regard to comparison between before and now, i.e. without memory and without any consciousness of the change, i.e. of the development as 'learning'), then a portfolio constitutes an interesting medium for the observation of changes of self. In other words, the portfolio makes it easier to separate learning from development and/or socialisation.

Already through this the portfolio constitutes a medium which makes it possible to observe second order knowledge. Of course one observes 'facts' first and foremost, i.e. world observations in the form of sound, image and text, but one also observes 'facts' in a temporal sequence between before and now. What is relevant to add to the already recorded knowledge of the world? What do I know today that I did not know yesterday? In other words, the portfolio makes it possible to observe learning.

But it must be added to this that the student always also has to reflect upon what private knowledge should be made accessible in the public knowledge space. When is the knowledge I have accumulated and elaborated relevant as a source for other people's knowledge? When is it worked into a form that can be passed on to the teacher? To carry out these operations, the student has to place him/herself in the place of the other, whether this other is the other students or the teacher. This stimulates the student to observe his/her own knowledge from the outside, i.e. in relation to the collective knowledge system represented by the class, or in relation to the knowledge system of teaching represented by the teacher.

There could be a particular public space, which could be called the 'assessment' or 'career selection' room. Here the student makes the material that he/she wishes to put forward for assessment available for observation and communication. The implicit precondition for doing so is for the student to judge when the knowledge generated by him/herself corresponds to the education system's expectations of acquisition of knowledge. In other words, the student has to place him/herself in the position of the system and observe him/herself through its horizon of expectations.

	Private	Student-student public	Student-teacher public
Observa-tion	Observation of material (observation of world representation, i.e. first order observation)	Observation of development of the other (observation of collective learning)	Observation of expectations of the educational system (observation of learning expectations)
Reflec-tion	Self-reflection: Observation of material in a before/after perspective (observation of individual learning, i.e. second order observation)	Comparative observation of the 'I' in the I/you relationship: 'I' observed through the collective other, i.e. third order observation in the I/you context.	Comparative observation of 'I' in the I/system relationship: 'I' observed through the education system, i.e. third order observation in a systemic context

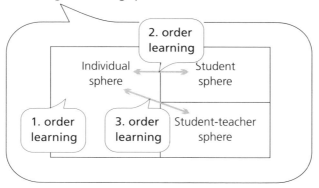

Conclusion

In this chapter I have argued for the following conclusions:

Firstly, I have argued that the current situation of e-learning in Europe is hampered by a lack of theoretical clarity. There exist at least four mutually incompatible and normally non-explicated paradigms.

Each one has its specific criterion of success and failure, and its specific understanding of the nature of ICT as a tool or medium for teaching and learning. I do not claim that theoretical consensus can or should be reached, but I do suggest that theoretical conditions should be made explicit.

Secondly, I have argued that the understanding of the relationship between ICT and teaching/learning depends on whether ICT is conceived of from a tool or media perspective. I argued in the chapter that teaching should be conceptualised as a specialised form of communication. This implies that the media perspective is the most relevant. This also implies that simple views of causality cannot explain the effect the new media have on teaching. It is therefore not reasonable to apply a simple cost-benefit consideration to e-learning.

Finally, I have tried to illustrate that in a teaching and research context it is appropriate to conceive of the new technologies as knowledge technologies and to apply the knowledge theoretical communication paradigm to e-learning. In this way it becomes possible to differentiate different forms of knowledge and processes of knowing. As I have demonstrated, this presupposes distinctions between forms of knowledge, which are different in nature. This might constitute a basis for e-learning analyses and evaluations across existing, incompatible theories.

5. Society's Educational System

– An Introduction to Niklas Luhmann's Pedagogical Theory[1]

Introduction

In chapters one to four the basic concepts of knowledge, learning and teaching have been presented and categorised, the field of media pedagogy has been critically analysed, and the phenomenon of digitally mediated education – e-learning – has been elaborated. However, all these chapters have been inspired and informed by Niklas Luhmann's theory of society, and particularly by his theory of knowledge (cf. Luhmann 1990) and of teaching, learning and education. Consequently, I found it adequate to devote this last chapter to an introduction to Luhmann's theory of society's educational system.

In the spring of 2002, probably the last large manuscript of Niklas Luhmann, who died in 1998 at the age of 70, was published. The manuscript is an almost completely developed analysis of the educational system of contemporary society. The book is entitled *Das Erziehungssystem der Gesellschaft*. Despite the fact that the work is one of many analyses of the differentiated functional systems of contemporary society, it is not only one book in a series, but is also based on Luhmann's lifelong interest in educational issues, which, among other things, is expressed in a series of books published in 1982, 1986, 1990, 1992 and 1996, which he edited together with Karl Eberhard Schorr: *Zwischen Technologie und Selbstreferenz, Zwischen Intransparenz und Verstehen, Zwischen Anfang und Ende, Zwischen Absicht und Person* and *Zwischen System und Umwelt*. In addition, in 1997, he published a book with Dieter Lenzen entitled *Bildung und Weiterbildung im Erziehungs-*

---

1. In this chapter all page references to Luhmann's *Das Erziehungssystem der Gesellschaft* are put in brackets without further reference. All quotes from this book have been translated by me.

system. In this chapter, *Das Erziehungssystem der Gesellschaft* is introduced; it is put into the context of Luhmann's total oeuvre; and it is related to the situation and function of education in our modern, "hypercomplex" society (cf. Qvortrup 1998 and 2003).

Background

Niklas Luhmann was appointed professor at the then new Bielefeld University in 1968, at the age of 40. His previous university career had been short. It was not until 1965 that he was appointed head of department in the social research centre in Dortmund, and in 1966 he wrote his dissertation and habilitated in Münster. This was preceded by a career in the public sector (cf. Horster 1997 and Reese-Schäfer 1992).

When starting to work at Bielefeld, he had to fill out one of the employee evaluation forms that were new at the time, but that have become standard procedure today. It was, after all, necessary to define "result goals" on which to base a measurement of future activities. His answers to three general questions were as follows:

– "Forschungssprojekt? Social theory."
– "Dauer? Thirty years."
– "Kosten? Keine!"[2]

During his first years of employment, Luhmann outlined the project of developing a social theory, i.e. a general theory of society, and completed the preliminary work, being especially inspired by Talcott Parsons, the American functionalist sociologist. After several large monographs, he started on two series, for which he wrote all the contributions: *Soziologische Aufklärung* was his theoretical laboratory and grew into six large volumes. *Gesellschaftsstruktur und Semantik* was a collection of knowledge sociological studies about subjects such as: the self-definition of the European upper class during the 17th and 18th century, the concept of time, the comprehension of European culture, legal consciousness, ideas of education and upbringing, historical

---

2. Luhmann tells this story himself in the preface to the work *Die Gesellschaft der Gesellschaft* (Luhmann 1997, p. 11).

concepts of nature, changing definitions of the ruling class, politics, religion, ethics, etc. Four volumes were published in this series and one book on the concept of love in Europe starting in the 13th century, *Liebe als Passion* (Luhmann, 1982). He already presented the motto of all these works – the programme declaration for a system of critical theory – in his inaugural lecture in 1967, which to a great extent demonstrated an ironical attitude toward the type of critical theory that is based on normative standards, and which, in its social analysis, focuses more on what society is not and what ideals it does not correspond to than what society is and why it is this way: "More preaching and threatening is not necessary, neither is the spread of obedience and reasonableness, rather the dominant theme will be the exposure and discrediting of official facades, ruling moral concepts and common beliefs" (Luhmann 1970, p. 69). Reification may also be socially relevant and not just the expression of "false consciousness", he added as a sharp comment against critical theory. Also notions of virtue and reasonableness are notions in society about which normative requirements are expressed in words and, therefore, these cannot simply be brought out into the open as universal normative expectation. Also Marxism, which claims to present the truth about society and to expose ideology and false beliefs, must know how to explain its claims to truth.

It was not until 1984, when Luhmann was 56, that the first work on social theory of his great research project concerning a theory of society appeared. The name of the book was *Soziale Systeme*. I remember how, in 1987 – or was it 1988 – I spent the whole summer deciphering incomprehensible expressions. The pages were filled with strange words like "autopoiesis", "self-reference", "distinction" and "interpenetration". The author made a distinction between "psychic systems" and "social systems" and asserted that psychic systems do not comprise a society's essence and building blocks but rather its surrounding world. Society is not a sum total of human individuals. Slowly I understood that this enabled one to create a theoretically based alternative to the opinion that the will of the people is a certain type of essence, a total of individual wishes, which in turn forms the basis for democracy. Thus, the book provided the reader with the understanding that the precondition for social order isn't a certain centripetal power: A public will, an omnipotent government, "capital" as a blind social force, or any other Archimedean point of observation. No, also highly complex, polycentric conglomerates of mutually loosely coupled systems may create social order, i.e. may constitute a meaning-based distinction between itself and its environment.

But even more importantly, the book turned upside-down the by then standard paradigms of society, organisation, communication, order, government, evolution, and of the relationship between human beings and society. It is hard today to understand the way in which – and the radicalism with which – both ontological and epistemological beliefs suddenly collapsed.

In other words, Luhmann thereby created an alternative to the fundamental question of how social order is possible. Social order is not created when a prince with his princely power, the state with its state power or the people with its will binds the society's atoms together into a whole. No, social order is established when the diversity of communicative systems creates an extremely complex and dynamic stability. Society does not exist on the strength of the purity of social order but rather on the complex impurity of social structures.

One of the book's main ideas was that society is not longer divided into layers with one ruling centre, but that it should be described as a functionally differentiated society, which consists of a large number of functional systems, each of which justifies itself: an economic system, legal system, art system, political system, religious system, etc., etc. At the same time, these multiple functional systems are not in mutual harmony. Quite the opposite, they constantly collide: they influence each other, modify each other and attempt to achieve dominance over each other; still, however, they are preconditions for each other and together form a whole that can be called society. It is no longer possible to refer to the one and only centre of a society. Society is polycentric, or "polycontextural" as characteristically expressed by Luhmann, since in a polycentric society each functional system creates its own surroundings, its own context. Several systems together, however, create a "semantic horizon" which represents the boundaries of what we understand and what is accessible to us, as opposed to that which remains on the other side of the semantic horizon. This is not "meaningless" (since meaninglessness also possesses meaning – even if it is negative), but is just beyond meaning.

During his entire career, Luhmann emphasised that the fact that society is polycentric does not mean that social theory, critical system theory, is "postmodern". This does not relax the requirement for truth. The statement that society is polycentric does not mean that many truths, and therefore none, exist. Quite the opposite, it is necessary to toughen the requirement for truth: every observation, at least those that claim to be scientific, must not only prove that which it observes. It must also prove the appropriateness of its observation process, that is, it must include "autological" elements (cf. Luhmann 1997, p. 16). No one has been more acute toward the lax postmodern viewpoint that "anything goes" than Luhmann.

As a systematician, Luhmann had no alternative: The theory on society had to include descriptions of the most important of the many functional systems. By his mid sixties, Luhmann had published large monographs on the economic system, the scientific system, the legal system and the art system. A preparatory work on the analysis of society's mass media, with the characteristically ambiguous title of *Die Realität der Massenmedien,* the reality of mass media, was published in 1996. At the same time, he felt that his strength was waning. The tremendous workload had exhausted him. "When I wake in the morning and feel pain in my body," he said in an interview "I know that I am not dead yet." Therefore, although his project could be entered in the public accounting as *"keine Kosten"*, its cost was one life.

Just at that time, in the mid 1990s, he therefore started his last project – the book that was to complete his grand oeuvre. His entire project, the goal of which was to work out a theory about society, contained three main components from the outset: the theoretical basis of social systems, which was published in 1984, books about the functional systems of society, of which four had been published between 1988 and 1995, and the final work, a book about how society as a society is formed, when the person observing society does not accept a position on the other side of society, but is always as an observer placed somewhere within the society that he/she describes. There is not such a thing as a position outside society. Consequently, the title could not be *"Die Gesellschaft"*, implying the existence of an external observer, but had to be *Die Gesellschaft der Gesellschaft:* Society observed from inside, i.e. society observed from a position within itself. The resulting 1,200-page work on society, which has already become a main work of contemporary sociology, was published before his death.

At the same time, in spite of this colossal work, a large number of functionally differentiated systems were still not described. Therefore, Luhmann further increased his work load and worked simultaneously on the analysis of three other of society's functional systems: a book about society's religion, one on society's politics and one on its educational system. And finally, he believed that it was necessary to write a book about that type of social systems that lies between society at large and the infinite number of small interaction systems, i.e. between sociology's macro and the micro level, as it is normally phrased. This type of social system in between society and the many interaction systems is: organisations. The nearly completed book manuscripts on religions, politics and education, as well as the book on organisation, *Organisation und Entscheidung* were handed over to a younger generation of Luhmannians, and they have all been published to date. The last one, the book about society's educational system, was brought to the printer by Luhmann's young colleague, Dieter Lenzen, and it was published, as already mentioned, in the spring of 2002.

Luhmann's conceptual system

Luhmann's project was a colossal 30-year research project, and when he wrote 350 pages on the economic system or 580 pages on the legal system, the goal was also to prove a general hypothesis that across the numerous different functional systems certain formal similarities exist.

In this respect the analyses of society's functional systems can be understood as a theoretical experiment. In the book *Social Systems* Luhmann developed an enormous system of mutually interrelated concepts. He so to speak elaborated a counter-intuitive description language. It is through this system of concepts that Luhmann analyses modern society and its individual functional systems, knowing that some phenomena will be seen clearly, while others will fade away in the background. The main result is that a different picture of society will emerge.

In the introduction to *Social Systems* Luhmann – both self-ironical and coy – presents a list of more than 35 concepts, which represent that conceptual machinery through which society can be observed. In relation to the book about society's educational system the most important concepts are: Communication, operative closure (self-reference, autopoiesis) and structural coupling. From these basic concepts other concepts such as media and code, and complexity and contingency can be defined.

A basic assumption of Luhmann's social theory is that society is not made of persons or actions, but of communication. According to Luhmann communication can be defined as coordinated selectivity. Something is selected, other things are excluded. One example is the classroom as a communication system. Through her choice of themes the teacher selects something, while other possibilities are excluded. Continuing the communication one can contribute to the same theme or suggest a new one. Consequently, one can connect to the ongoing communication, or one can disconnect from it.

This implies that the concepts of "operative closure" and "structural coupling" become central. Both the communication system and the psychic system are operatively closed. In the way in which they operate, they constitute their own elements. When I look at my neighbour's apple tree, the apples do not fly through the air into my consciousness. No, those apples, which I see, are products of the operations of my own psychic system. Luhmann also uses the concepts of self-reference and autopoiesis – self-production – about this phenomenon.

But does this imply that no contact exists between the systems? No, but "contact" should not be perceived as a causal relationship, but as – structural coupling. Partly one system can provide resources for another system, partly it can limit the other system's operational potentials. For instance, the brain as a neural system is a resource for consciousness: Without a neural system we could not think. But at the same time the brain limits the operational potentials of our consciousness: For instance we can hear some sounds and not others. Still, however, it is not the brain, but the consciousness that thinks. No concepts, only neural signals, float around in the brain. Consequently, the relationship between these mutually closed systems should be called a relationship of structural coupling.

This is also the case for the relationship between human beings and social systems. The communication in the classroom cannot "penetrate" into the consciousness of the pupils. No matter how clearly and convincingly the teacher talks, she cannot talk into the head of the individual child. Like the apples in my neighbour's garden, communication does not fly through the air into the consciousness. Still, communication cannot exist without psychic systems and vice versa. Thus, structural couplings can and will emerge. The classroom as a social system and the child as a psychic system are mutually closed. But they provide complexity – resources and limitations – for each other. Classroom communication is a resource for and a limitation of the learning of the child, and the consciousness of the child is a resource for and a limitation of classroom communication. This implies that the operational potential of the teacher is to communicate and to organise communication. She cannot learn for or on behalf of the child, and she cannot create any causal effects. The teacher communicates and orchestrates communication, the children learn – but structural couplings will emerge.

Functional differentiation: media, code, self-reference

As a result of the fact that any social system is based on communication and is self-referential, that is, operationally closed, it must observe the surrounding world through a specific medium that the system in question has itself created. This medium is based on a specific code. Also, every single functionally differentiated system creates its own symbolic generalisation. Partly, the symbolically generalised medium raises the potential success level of a specific functional system's communication. Partly, however, by raising the potential success level the functional system also increases the risk that misinformation will be created by the communication.

These concepts – medium, code, symbolic generalisation – thus represented elements of the assumptions concerning the nature of these functionally differentiated social systems, and in order to prove his theory, Luhmann must answer the question regarding what the specific medium and code is for each individual functional system, and he must analyse the impacts concerning efficiency and risk of misinformation for each system.

For example, the medium for the economic system is money and the code is payment/non-payment. Therefore purchasing at any discount supermarket is so effective. Just put the merchandise on the checkout line, the cashier calculates the price and money – represented by metal, paper or electronic bytes – changes ownership. No words are needed. However, if one wants to communicate other things than buying and selling commodities, it will most likely be misunderstood. Try, for example, to declare love to the cashier. He or she will most likely misunderstand your communicative selections and call for the boss to help you out.

Similarly, the medium of the political system is power and the code is power over non-power. Some believe that our political world is based on the sum of rational choices of politicians and voters. In reality, this is only part of the truth. Alliances are created in parties. Rhetorical methods are used, threats and promises are made and agreements drawn up. One party leader is overthrown by the next and political positions are distributed according to power criteria (not so much according to professional relevance), and although more words are used than when making purchases at the discount supermarket, the logic is the same: the range of communicative variations is reduced, thus increasing efficiency, but also raising the risk of excluding relevant communicative selections. In simpler terms, we could say that everyone knows what, to a lesser or greater extent, is behind all the nice words – power! And this naturally means that certain things can only be expressed with difficulty, for instance beautiful and loveable messages. Because one can assume that even in the case of the most loveable means of expression, the lust for power is hidden within.

The fact that the functional systems are operationally closed, does not exclude that they possess certain functions in relation to the society as a whole and perform certain services in relation to individual occurrences in society. On the contrary: They are so effective because they are operationally closed. The function of the economic system is the reduction of deficiencies. The service is to satisfy needs. And the fact that this system possesses this function and provides the specified service is not dependent on the fact that is directed by an external higher logic, *deus ex machina* or world soul. Quite the opposite: the fact that the economic system is operationally closed, without taking others into consideration, contains the condition of its functionality.

There are enough examples to demonstrate that the elimination of this operational isolation in favour of a political or scientific distribution does not reduce shortcomings, but rather increases them.

Another example is the mass media system. Its code is +/- information: What counts e.g. as news, what does not? Its reflection system or form of self-description is journalistic criteria, etc. Its function in society, i.e. to "irritate" society and to keep it awake, is based on the fact that it is functionally closed: It is not directed by any external power, but selects information, e.g. news, according to its own criteria. The same goes for its service, e.g. to create a transcendental illusion of a common world. These functions and services have not been created by a metaphysical authority (by which the mass media system is promoted as a "fifth state authority" and similar lyrical expressions). No, these are based on the autopoietic power and the resulting structural couplings.

This does not mean that this complex of differentiated functional systems represents the best of all worlds. Luhmann does not offer utopia, but a cynical description of society. The way in which these autopoietic systems work, that is "...the growth dynamic characteristic of contemporary society and the channelling of this growth through individual functional systems, especially economics, science, education and politics", is a constant source of social problems. "All these systems are structurally stipulated to deviate from planned results. They follow individual growth and improvement objectives. It is not possible to grasp the internal effects for society of these dynamics. The increase in regional differences combined, at the same time, with global interdependence is perhaps the most noticeable fact." (Luhmann 1988, p.169f, my translation LQ)

Even more imposing are the ecological effects, Luhmann pointed out as early as in 1988: "In our time, probably the most central problem of contemporary society is the feedback-results for society of the changes unleashed by it on the surrounding world. This does not apply only to the physical-chemical-organic environment; to the same extent this applies to the social system in relation to the physical surroundings. Our social system is changing the living conditions on earth to an extent never before seen." (Luhmann 1988, p. 169, my translation)

The characterisation of Luhmann as a "neo-conservative" as

Habermas has done on several occasions, is not fair. But Luhmann's goal wasn't to moralise. There is no purpose in describing the world the way it ought to be, when there is such a great need to describe it as it actually functions. And this is the precondition for doing critical theory. True critical theory must be contra-intuitive, also in relation to that kind of emancipatory theory, which in its emancipatory beliefs defeats all competitors in conservatism.

Das Erziehungssystem der Gesellschaft: A system's theory of education

Luhmann's descriptions of society's functional systems, therefore, are based on a background that is, concurrently, strongly directed by theory and with a strong empirical orientation. He wants to describe social systems as they are, not as one would like that they should be and therefore are not, and this requires a strong empirical orientation. But he also wants to describe them in opposition to the assumptions caused by conventional wisdom, and this requires strong theory. On this basis, the books dealing with functionally differentiated systems provide two major scientific contributions:

1. They present contra-intuitive re-descriptions of individual functional systems, descriptions that, being strictly based on concepts, avoid all the traditional lyricism and ingrained assumptions. Since they are based on concepts, they are not sentimental, but rather, as some have put it, almost cynical.
2. They present actualised re-descriptions of different functional systems, descriptions that are actualised since they are strictly based on the presumption that society is functionally differentiated and that a basic social challenge is contingency, that is, the multitude of possibilities for establishing communication within society. Therefore, the basic presumption is not that society should be characterised by stratification. The basic presumption is also not that society should be characterised by being divided into simple opposites – between good and evil, progressive and conservative, profane and sacred, or work and capital. No, a basic presumption is that social systems develop in order to cope with external com-

plexities, and that they do so by increasing their internal complexity, which again provide increased external complexity for other differentiated functional systems.

I would like to focus on these two contributions when I present the most important contributions to pedagogical theory of the book *Das Erziehungssystem der Gesellschaft.*

However, a terminological problem must be mentioned: the German word *"Erziehung"* includes both "upbringing" and "education". The background for this is that *"Erziehungsfunktionen"* were functionally differentiated in the 18th and 19th century respectively into upbringing and public education. Among other things, Luhmann's book also analyses this differentiation process, and consequently it deals with upbringing as well as education. In English, the title of the book should therefore be "The upbringing-and-educational system of society". In the following text, I have generally translated the concept of *"Erziehung"* as "education".

The need for a system's theory of education

Generally what applies in the case of functional systems in society is that the more they are differentiated, the more they must base themselves on their own self-reasoning. The result is that the need for theories for these systems increases in step with their movement toward independence. Economic theories grow out of "tableaux économiques" forms from the 17th century, that is, models and theories about the self-reproductive character of economic systems. These theories culminate, in some sense, in Karl Marx's theory about the accumulation and circulation of capital, that is, capital as an autopoietic system (according to Bob Jessop), the effectiveness of which is increased according to how negligently – that is, self-indicatively – they function. Political theories develop as an extension of Machiavelli's rationale of 16th century politics as an independent decision-making system, again with the implication that negligence and performance are downright proportional.

The fact that these systems are autopoietic does not mean that they lack contact with the surrounding world. Quite the opposite – it is the self-reference of a system that makes it possible for it to establish contact with its environment, while also preserving itself as a system. Thereby, on the one hand, an interpenetrational relationship can be created between the system and the surrounding world, that is, the system can define the surrounding world as a resource for the maintenance of the system. On the other hand, a structural coupling relationship can be established between the system and the surrounding work, which means that the system can thematise the surrounding world as information or irritation in regard to the preservation of the system, and thereby examine the question as to uncertainty and adaptive self-preservation.

Similarly, a theory on the educational system as a system which cannot be understood just as a residual of the modus operandi of other social systems is strongly needed, cf. the attempts in the 1970s to develop a theory about the "political economics of the educational sector". The core of such a theory is a concept of education and study, that is, pedagogy. One such theory was articulated by Rousseau, see his book "Emile" on upbringing, and by Kant in his posthumously published pedagogical writings. But to a certain extent, only after the proposal to treat education as a differentiated, autopoietic functional system the theory of the educational system can be raised to the same level as theories about other functional systems in society. In retrospect, it can be said that this was the aim of Luhmann's pedagogical writings in the 1980s and 1990s, which culminated in the work, *Das Erziehungssystem der Gesellschaft,* in 2002.

Like the other functional systems, the educational system also creates an interpenetrational relationship between the system and its surrounding world as well as a structural coupling relationship. The educational system, on the one hand, observes the surrounding world – the political system, the economic system, current and future students – as a potential resource. This represents the interpenetrational relationship. On the other hand, the educational system creates a structural coupling relationship between the system and the environment. In this case, the educational system views the surrounding world as a potential irritant: it registers threats of interference from political and economic systems, or threats to the problem-free preservation of the educational system from current or future students (ill-bred or poorly socialised ones). Children are therefore always seen as pupils or students in the educational system, and these students are defined intermittently as teachable children (resource) and risk children (threat).

Preliminary work

As already mentioned, in 1982, 1986, 1990, 1992 and 1996, Luhmann, together with Karl Eberhard Schorr, published a series of collections of articles about upbringing and education: *Zwischen Technologie und Selbstreferenz* (Between technology and self-reference), *Zwischen Intransparenz und Verstehen* (Between intransparency and understanding), *Zwischen Anfang und Ende* (Between beginning and end), *Zwischen Absicht und Person* (Between purpose and person) and *Zwischen System und Umwelt* (Between system and environment). In addition, after the death of Schorr, in 1997, Luhmann published a book together with Dieter Lenzen entitled *Bildung und Weiterbildung im Erziehungssystem* (Education and further education in the educational system).

The starting point for all these books is the educational system, and each of them analyse a specific dilemma of this system: The book about technology[3] and self-reference deals with the dilemma that teachers must, on the one hand, assume that they are capable of changing the children to be taught. In other words, the teacher acts in a systematic, teleological, manner that is technological. On the other hand, the teacher can never think that the person being taught is his/her handiwork: the teacher brings up and teaches a free being (a self-referential being) until its independence.

The book about non-transparency and understanding deals with the dilemma that the teacher and the student try to understand each other, to create that which Habermas called mutual comprehension, while at the same time they are mutually non-transparent.

The book about beginning and end deals both with the uncertainty of teaching – that which is located between two definite points, between the start and the finish – and with being constantly between the starting point, which had a purpose, and the finishing line, the result of which deviates from the initial purpose. Thus, the book analy-

---

3. The concept of "technology" is the concept for the causal relationships that are the basis of intentional activities and to which those actions must be aligned that are supposed to have practical effects.

ses the basics of didactics, defining didactics as the art of structuring the time between beginning and end of a course or lecture.

The book about purpose and person deals – again – with the intentionality of the relationship, that is, between the movement toward the goal and the unforeseen result, here expressed in the relationship that teaching brings out the individual as a person, that is as somebody who is capable of relating to him/herself as something other than him/herself. If it succeeds, education maintains and forms non-trivial psychic systems that are capable of making distinctions, and can view themselves as malleable, that is, as individuals.

Finally, the book about the relationship between system and environment deals with the fact that teaching means the surmounting of boundaries between the pupil as a psychic system and teaching as a communications system. Again, we are dealing with a project that constitutes the sine qua non of teaching, yet is also an impossible one, because this boundary is insurmountable.

The final volume, *Bildung und Weiterbildung im Erziehungssystem*, which is a collection of articles from 1997, can be treated as a preliminary work to *Das Erziehungssystem der Gesellschaft*. The topics treated include lifelong learning, and Luhmann modifies some of his earlier statements, for instance, about identifying the social construction of "the child" as the symbolically generalised medium of the educational system. Instead, it is suggested that in a society characterised by lifelong learning the concept of "life process", in German *"Lebenslauf"*, should replace "the child" as symbolic generalisation.

The function of society's educational system

As all other monographs about one function system, the book dealing with the educational system of the society includes, on the one hand, the characterisation of the functional system with the help of a collection of general concepts that for many at the first instance seem to be strange and even "queer", but that because of their strangeness allow a series of acute and unsentimental observations about the functional system in question. This represents a fundamental surplus of Niklas Luhmann's scientific contribution: Just the strangeness of the system theoretical concepts makes it possible to create new observations, since we naturally see the world differently through newly polished optics than we do through the eye-glass(es) of habit and traditions.

What is the idea of an educational system? As already mentioned, earlier opticians have offered the idea that an educational system must maintain some definite instructional standard, to reproduce the "capital relationship" as it was called at one time, etc. But if we try to look beyond such statements based on social semantics that is based on questionable general applicability, according to Luhmann we reach the general conclusion that the function of the educational system is to change people in the direction of definite goals. "Speaking about education (upbringing/education, LQ), one primarily thinks about intentional activities that try to develop a person's abilities and foster his/her ability for social communion" (p. 15).

Does this sound self-evident? If yes, Luhmann adds a very quick objection: How is it possible "to change people"? Seemingly, there is a clear causal relationship in this: the subject does something with the object so that the object changes. But this involves at least three problems. How does one determine the goal of the educational system? Who is the object of this change process? And how is this change process actually realised, i.e. which tools are available?

The purpose of the educational system: cultivation as contingency formula

Firstly, we must ask who is the subject, who is acting and how does he/she know what the goal of the action is? Is the family who is bringing up a child the subject of the upbringing and education? And to the extent that upbringing and education is a familial activity, it can be asked how does the family identify the goals? Something similar also applies to the educational system. What must a child know at specific ages? Can politicians determine this? Or developmental psychologists? Parents? Teachers or pedagogues?[4] And how, despite the difficulty of the project, do they still arrive again and again at descriptions of the goals to which they attach applicability, calling them "definite goals", "general cultivation" or "educational canons"? Here

---

4. Here and hereafter I use the concept of "pedagogue" in its etymological, initial meaning, that is, as an indication of a specialised group that deal with pedagogy, that is, the art (theory) of upbringing and teaching.

Luhmann persuasively argues that the concept of "cultivation" is that which he calls a "contingency formula" (I will return to this concept), namely society's establishment of educational goals. As a contingency formula cultivation is a concept for something that cannot be specifically defined, but for which a word is needed that signals a mutual understanding and agreement. Therefore, cultivation, the contingency formula of the educational system corresponds to "God", the contingency formula of religion, or to the well known phrase of researchers, that "further research is needed", the contingency formula of science. All these concepts are a kind of communication tricks that allow communication to continue despite the lack of metaphysical security.

The object of the educational system: the human being as a conglomerate of non-trivial systems

Secondly, we could ask, who is the object of the change process of education, this human being who is to be modelled in order to achieve some definite goal? Maybe it is here that we can find the decisive non-self-evidence of upbringing and education. Because what is "a human being"? A human being is not a trivial machine. In other words, it is not some system that upon definite input through a specific function discharges some definite output. Furthermore, a human being is not just a non-trivial system, but even a conglomerate of non-trivial systems, a highly complex system in which a constant reproduction of self-distinctions takes place, as Luhmann says. Luhmann characterises such "machines"[5] with uncommon ontological characteristics as follows: "They operate with the help of built-in reflection loops, which adapt all the input/output transformations to the actual condition of the machine; or more exactly: after such an actual historical condition into which the machine has brought itself. Since this condition changes with each operation, these machines have at their disposal a practically limitless, at least uncalculated repertoire of reaction possibilities." (p. 77). These are therefore the conglomerates of non-trivial, unforeseen systems, which educators and

---

5. This metaphor is taken from the Austrian-American systems theoretician Heinz von Foerster. However, it also ironically refers to the implicit expectations of the educational system that teaching has causal effects.

teachers must change without clearly defined goals – using communication as the only resource.

As it turns out, education as a field, namely to change human beings, is correctly understood as an extremely non-self-evident project. As Luhmann writes on p. 82: "If we are to comprehend individual people as conglomerates of autopoietic, self-dynamic, non-trivial systems, this doesn't prove any motive for the opinion that they can be brought up/cultivated." The only existing resources are structural couplings between instruction as communications, on the one hand, and psychic systems, on the other hand. Hereby Luhmann cuts through simplifications which were brought forth by descriptions of behavioural causality (which do not see the autonomy of learning as a problem at all), but also through those fog clouds which have been produced by those learning theories which have expanded learning to everything – even to that which would otherwise be described as teaching – and which, therefore, do not have concepts for identifying the necessary structural coupling between the communications system (teaching) and the psychic system (the learning system).

As opposed to learning theory, which implicitly unites teachers and students into one and the same element of the learning process, Luhmann's concepts bring out the asymmetric role of teaching: some teach, that is, communicate. Others learn, that is, they couple themselves to the teaching communication. This specifically implies that Marx's famous expression that the educator is also educated may be further refined: the educator educates – and may therefore be socialised.

Taken specifically, this asymmetric communication means that "Wahrnehmung des Wahrgenommenswerden" is an essential aspect of the student's role in the teaching communication. As a non-trivial system, every student learns to become aware of the observation of him/herself. And in the same way, the majority of teachers learn to observe students with the knowledge that they are aware of being observed.

In his characteristically ironic side-comments, Luhmann asserts that this understanding of a structural coupling between teaching (the communication process of the classroom) and learning (the mental process of the pupil or student) means that the problem of the trivialisation of teaching need not be taken as seriously, as it is usually done: because "... what happens when non-trivial systems find themselves in situations where they participate in trivialisation? They attune themselves for this through self-socialisation. Or in other words: they learn to handle it. They build a reflection loop within themselves, which makes clear to them the conditions under which it is advisable to act as a trivial system."(p. 79). And this also has long-term beneficial prospects because "...thereby, in set situations, non-trivial systems learn to act as trivial ones, without identifying themselves with this possibility." (p. 80). Thereby one learns to imagine, that is, to develop a personal identity policy without identifying oneself with the situation with which one become attuned.

The one and only resource of teaching: communication

Thirdly, one could ask, what is the resource – i.e. the medium – of teaching? The answer is that the only way in which upbringing and teaching can take place is with the help of communication. Socialisation may take place as an activity that is copied. But the one who brings up and teaches is directed to communicate, and the child must observe those activities, which are copied. Also, in the class room the teacher must communicate and organise communications. He may talk to the children, make drawings on the blackboard, walk around from pupil to pupil, help and support, observe what the children are doing, correct written homework, organise group work, etc. etc. Always, teaching is communication.

Generally speaking, this communication takes place in interaction groups, regardless of whether the interaction is that of Rousseau's dialogue between the educator and Emile, who is to be educated, or that which takes place in a school system's classrooms. In any case, this communication takes place between reciprocally present people. Therefore Luhmann makes the following proposal for, as he calls it, a quasi-tautological definition of cultivation/education: "As education (cultivation/education, LQ) all communications must apply which are actualised as interactions in order to educate." (p. 54).

If this definition is accepted, it implies, among other things, that e-learning, e.g. distance education, is also interaction, that is, communication between those present. E-learning does use distribution media other than seeing and listening, that is light and sound waves as communication media in the classroom, but despite this, it can be described as interaction. Otherwise, it would not be teaching. It is however obvious that e-learning provides very special and in many senses very restricted media to teaching interaction. Consequently, e-learning – actually, the correct name is e-teaching – can be described as teaching that uses other distribution media than those available in the ordinary classroom to establish communicative relations between reciprocally present people. Sometimes, the interaction of e-learning is synchronous, at other times it is asynchronous. Sometimes, the interaction takes place in a geographically restricted group, at other times the e-learning system covers large distances. Sometimes, the interaction medium only allows for written communication, in other situations oral and visual communication is made possible. Still, however, e-learning is communication between those present for each other through the digital media of the e-learning system.

Communication media of the educational system

Every communication or observation takes place through some media. When we observe someone – also some who is physically present – this takes places through media: through air, which facilities hearing, with the help of light, which makes seeing possible.

According to Luhmann, the function of communication media is to reduce the improbability of communication. Generally speaking the success of communications is improbable. If this improbability is not as great as it usually should be, then this is the effect of the communication media.

In its fundamental form, the communication of the educational system takes place in the classroom as interaction between the students and teacher or teachers that are present. This communication is characterised, as is all other communications, by three improbabilities. The first improbability is that one will hear what the other is saying. The teacher tries, sometimes without results, to have a say and make the students direct their attention to what he/she is saying. The second improbability is that one understands what the other is saying. The teacher asks the students to pay attention and they do not understand what he/she means. The third and last improbability is that the communications achieve the striven-for effect. The students hear and maybe also understand, but do not change their behaviour.

In correspondence with these three improbabilities, Luhmann identifies three types or aspects of communication media.[6]

The first type is distribution media: the teacher does not whisper but raises his/her voice. In order for the students to hear and see better, the teacher stands higher up and writes important words on the blackboard, uses overhead projector slides, PowerPoint presentations or computer-based communication. In order to reach parents, letters and notices are sent home to the family.

The second type is comprehension media. Language is one of the fundamental comprehension media; a conceptual vocabulary and reference system is another. Curriculum work and instruction planning consists of creating a purposeful development of comprehension media in the classroom.

The third type is effect media. The function of this media is to achieve the intended effect. This is achieved with rhetorical resources, with the creation of togetherness in the classroom, with the teacher acting "authentically", and fundamentally with having the students acquire the specialised communication media of the educational system, that is, the comprehension that the aim of education is the acquisition of knowledge, and that this knowledge will be tested with the help of tests and examinations.

Just as the educational system has developed reflection resources for itself as an educational system (didactic and pedagogical), it has also developed reflection resources for its communication media. This reflection system is called the theory of the means of instruction. Its history reaches back at least to Petrus Ramus's reflections on lectures as communication media and this achieved an early peak with Comenius's textbook and with the reflection of the textbook as a specialised communication media.

These days, there is an accelerating theory on e-learning and also a theory on how digital media can reduce the improbability of teaching communication, again in three ways:

— By overcoming time and space barriers.
— By making comprehension more likely, for instance with so-called

---

6. Cf. the analysis of the improbabilities of communication and the need for communication media in chapter three, above

programmed teaching, which supports the learning of the child by modifying the inputs as a result of the answers given by the child, or with the help of simulation programs.

– And finally, by increasing the probability of changing behaviour, for instance, with educational computer games and edutainment programs.

The primary function of an educational system: making human beings persons

According to Luhmann, the fundamental function of an educational system is not to impart knowledge, to discipline, etc., but to minimise the improbability of social communication. An educational system achieves this through the function of making human beings persons, that is, by creating that distinction, for which the labelled side is the person and the unlabelled side is the human being.

With the concept of "person", Luhmann indicates that empiric people can be generalised and thereby made communicative. Just think if, in our everyday communication, we had to take into consideration the empiric multi-facets of other human beings! This would make communication impossible. No, only the fact that it is possible to simplify, that is, to speak with one human being as a seller, another as a teacher, a third as a schoolchild, and a fourth as a beloved, makes communication possible. On the contrary, the fact that we as human beings are capable of plugging ourselves into some form of person, allows us to participate in communications. "This form..." defines Luhmann, "...which allows the system dynamics of individual human beings to be ignored in social communication, is indicated by the concept of 'person'." (p. 28). Therefore the "human being" is the unlabelled side of the person as form, and it is not human beings but persons that make communication possible.

The ability to communicate therefore does not assume, adds Luhmann unsentimentally, that other human beings are observed in their total multi-faceted complexity, but that things are simplified. On the one hand, the form "person" is the condition for the continuation of communication, it is an address, calculation point and often also an explanation for strange circumstances in the communication process. On the other hand, the form "person" is as well a product of the communication system. Summing up, "the person" is a communicative trick: a product of and a precondition for communication. When starting a new class I introduce myself as "your teacher" or as "professor of media research", thus leaving aside many other potential personal addresses. During my teaching this form or etiquette will be as well specified as modified: "your teacher" becomes "the busy teacher", "the nice/strange/absent-minded guy" etc. Still, however, these generalisations perform the trick of making communication possible.

Based on this, Luhmann presents a hypothesis that the primary function of the upbringing and education communication system is the transformation of human beings into persons: persons for themselves and for others:

> "Human beings are born. Persons develop through socialisation and upbringing/education. Keeping this difference in mind, it is natural to set the education function into relation with the fact that human beings become persons. Especially in complex societies, this cannot be left only to socialisation. This does not function specifically enough and is too connected to the environment where this occurs. In both instances we are dealing with the process of becoming a personality. It is here that leeway exists that education can use in order, on the one hand, to correct the results of socialisation, and on the other hand to amend them. But that interaction develops at all between socialisation and education depends on whether both processes are related to becoming a person." (p. 38).

This naturally does not mean that the education does not have other functions. However, these other functions are also connected to the formation of person, since the transformation of a child into a person increases the possibilities for the child of coupling to the social system. And this is what is achieved by bringing up and teaching a child to function as a *homme, citoyen and bourgeois*, that is, as a person, citizen and employee. These three categories have been the three dominating person types since the 18th century: a human being for other human beings, a citizen for the society and a competent employee in private and public institutions.

The secondary function of an educational system: career selection

More specifically, an educational system functions not only for up-bringing and cultivation, but also for career selection. Everyone does not have to do the same thing or fulfil the same function, and also this selection process is taken care of by the education system. Ergo, the educational system includes, no matter how much the participants protest, two functions: on the one hand, it functions to create and (to an increased degree in the form of lifelong education) to maintain the preconditions for human beings to function in society as persons. On the other hand, it functions to execute evaluations in order to realise career selection. Naturally, both functions have to be fulfilled by the educational system with the help of communication.

As it is known, educational systems have always had difficulties with its selection function because this is in conflict with the development of people's social skills. One increases the social coupling possibilities. The other limits them, since that human being, which develops into a number of persons in society, should not be made into all types of persons. Some selection needs to be made, and therefore this selection impacts negatively and even appears as suppression.

However, actually selection is not an antithesis to the development of person, but is the continuation of the project to make human beings more communicative. If we became "everything", our chances for participating in social communication, especially if we speak of contemporary and highly differentiated society, would be smaller than if a functional specification of that human being had taken place.

In addition, the career selection that takes place in a contemporary educational system is decidedly different from the selection that takes place in traditional societies. The selection that takes place, for instance, in the form of examination, is not an effect of socialisation, but of education. Therefore, selection helps social integration based on the past (family tree, social network, connections, traditions, etc.) to be replaced by social integration based on the future (that is, existing career potential) (cf. p. 69).

At the same time, it is important to note that the highly formalised examination form familiar from contemporary educational systems represents a "circular process", which influences both the contribution and the evaluation (p. 66). The answers given in the examination room affect the evaluation. However, it also has a feedback effect to the teaching contribution preceding the examination. Not only the student is evaluated but also the teacher, and therefore the examination allows for, or even intensifies, reflections on teaching (p. 67).

Finally, it should be noted that career selection based on examinations is separated from the use of power (p. 69), especially if examinations are highly formalised. A censor (or co-examiner), that is an external observer, participates in the examination and observes both the student and the teacher, and in order to prevent the use of power to an even greater degree, an appeal system has been developed. Therefore it can be stated polemically that these highly formalised forms of examination are not harmful but beneficial to students, if we leave aside that naturally they have a psychosocial effect which may be irritating.

The code of the educational system

As already mentioned, every functionally differentiated system must have a symbolically generalised medium and therefore a code for communication. Naturally this does not mean that the entire communications in an educational institution, for instance, takes place only in the code of this system, but this code moulds the communication and increases its potential for success. Everyone knows what is being talked about and therefore does not need many words, as in the previously described example of discount supermarket communication.

Earlier, Luhmann – inspired by Philippe Ariès's famous work on the social semantics of the concept of childhood (Ariès 1982) – has proposed that the symbolically generalised medium of an educational system is "the child" (see Luhmann 1991). Naturally, this concept of "child" does not denote a concrete, empiric child, but represents the generalisation of those empiric children in the educational system. Only on the basis of a generalisation of the child as such (from time to time "weak", from time to time "competent") and with the constant characterisation of his/her different phases of evolution (development psychology also tries with its phase-based specifications to offer generalisations) communication of the educational system is made possible. What do teachers talk about among themselves? About children! What do teachers and parents talk about, not when they meet at the discount supermarket or at the election precinct, but at the parent-teacher meeting? About the child! While the contingency formula was a communication trick of the aim of communication, the code is the communication trick of the double contingency of communication.

At the same time, the specific social semantic specification of the category child expresses the general function of the educational system: to change people. At least in earlier times, human beings – grown up human beings – were completed realities that were not possible to change. But children were and are just defined as that human being which can still be moulded. Faced by a challenge to do something intentional with the conglomerates of non-trivial systems (which is what empiric children are), this symbolic generalisation "child" creates a hope: the individual child is not, after all, what it will be, and it does not simply learn that which it learns, because it conducts those selections of understanding that it is determined to do. No, observing the teaching object through the media of "the child", teachers can "... understand the internal surplus production, the restlessness and movement and the self-transparency and self-created inconclusiveness that is created by their clients, as their own chance, since they treat children as a medium which make the creation of form possible. (...) The media "child" is thus not a specific child. It is a social construction that allows for the educator/teacher to believe that it is possible to educate and teach children." (p.91).

Despite this, in the work *Das Erziehungssystem der Gesellschaft* Luhmann abandons this proposition. In a society that is ever more characterised by lifelong education, the category of "child" does not work as an educational system medium. Rather, "human being" could be considered as symbolically generalised communication medium, if it is possible to identify some stabilised medium in the changing phase of a society's educational system, but "human being" with many of the social semantic characteristics that were previously assigned to "the child." This "human being", which forms a fundamental category in a society that holds lifelong learning to be an ideal, is an infantile human being, namely a human being that permits never-ending, continued moulding. A human being becomes an adult – and acquires supplemental training. A person retires – and has time to sit at a school bench again.

Since, however, the category of "human being" is already occupied, Luhmann, inspired by Dieter Lenzen (see Lenzen/Luhmann

1997) recommends using the category of *"Lebenslauf"*, i.e. lifetime or life process (see p. 93). It would seem that Luhmann thereby wishes to bring out the expressiveness and malleability that is not dependent on age, and that has become a lifelong characteristic in our society. But to me this proposal still does not sound convincing. It is presented with a good purpose and is well-founded. But it is not seen in an educational system, the way money is seen in stores and supermarkets, and power in the political system.

The code that corresponds to the media of "lifetime", according to Luhmann is transmittable/non-transmittable. A positive value of an educational system is namely that some allow themselves to be transmitted and that something is transmittable. But still, although the proposal is presented with good reason and actually represents the selfunderstanding of teachers, it is not very elegant.

Self-reflection of the educational system

Just as other function systems have reflection systems that have the purpose of reflecting what it is that gives the system a positive value (bookkeeping and budgets are used to ascertain how to make profits; the purpose of political programmes is to identify measures that may create power; theories and methods are the preconditions of scientific systems to guarantee positive value in the code +/- truth), the reflection system of an educational system is pedagogy. Pedagogy – and more specifically related to the different subjects: didactics – allows for teachers to reflect on how their communicative selections in the interaction system of the classroom may increase the probability of successful learning. Thereby, one also promotes the chances of positive values of secondary coding: better/worse. This is measured in the examination room and results in the above-mentioned career selection.

Generally, the rule applies, as mentioned above, that the more the function systems are differentiated, the more they must base themselves on their self-generated self-justification.

The result is that the educational system from having been based on standards (that is, defined by others) increasingly becomes self-justified, that is on self-reflection. Thus, pedagogy develops into a scientific discipline. "Concurrently with the disappearance of the conviction, that an indisputable scholarly standard exists, on which the teacher's authority could rest, unsolvable problems become visible. Pedagogy tries to establish itself as a science and to acquire the respective verbiage." (p. 192). Earlier upbringing and education could take place on the basis of standards. Upbringing and teaching were based on existing traditions and values. If, however, doubts occur about this basis, upbringing and teaching must be transferred to a reflective basis, that is to a scientific one. Why has the National Teacher's college been eliminated in Denmark, and a Danish Pedagogical University created? Because upbringing and teaching have started to doubt their own basis and must therefore study this basis – to be based on science, not traditions. Pedagogy has been transferred to the university, because society has become contingent.

More specifically, my proposal is that regarding the self-reflection of the educational system one should differentiate between first order and second order self-reflection. The first order of self-reflection is the direct reflection of teaching practices, that which Donald Schön calls the reflective practice of reflective practitioners. The systematisation of first order of teaching reflection is called didactics. This is related either to the teaching of special subjects, and in that case is called subject didactics, or with teaching generally, and in that case is called general didactics.

The second order of self-reflection is the indirect reflection of teaching practices, that is, the observation of the relationship between reflective relationship and the reflective practitioner and his practice. Here, the teacher reflects his immediate self-reflection. He reflects upon the basic assumptions, on which didactics is based. This second order of self-reflection is called pedagogy.

Das Erziehungssystem der Gesellschaft: a theory of society's educational system

The society in which we live is characterised by an abundance of opportunities. We have more opportunities that we are capable of realising or even pay attention to. This society is characterised by self-created uncertainty and insecurity. This basic characteristic expressed in professional sociological terminology is contingency: it creates an abundance of possibilities.

Such a society can be described in at least two opposing ways: on the one hand, it creates the impression of a society where everything is possible. All the illusion masters are here: those who have coined society a "learning society", and the so-called learning theoreticians, who wish to delete the concept of teaching, since teaching according to them creates limitations for the self-fulfilment of individuals and is therefore suppressive. No, only the concept of "learning" is legitimate, and the teacher's assignment is to stimulate this splendid learning, that is self-fulfilment and self-realisation.

On the other hand, such a society seems to be a society where nothing is assured. We have critics who speak about what heartbreaking and exhausting consequences are caused when no one ever says stop, no limits are set, and on the contrary, everyone can chase after their opportunities and this race never ends. This is treated by Richard Sennett's *The Corrosion of Character*, as well as many, many other books on social criticism.

However, my point is that the either-or position will not lead anywhere. Instead it is much more interesting to ascertain what kind of society produces/elicits these two positions, that is, to remain a bystander in the either-or argument. How is a society which is characterized by contingency, by an abundance of opportunities, constructed? And what are the consequences for a society that is constructed in this way?

Returning to an earlier mentioned concept, one can say that a fundamental function of such a society is to develop "contingency formulas", that is formulas that make possible the relation of oneself to the abundance of opportunities and their handling. But these formulas have very special characteristics. They cannot simply reduce the number of opportunities, that is, to say that you cannot do or get this, just as you cannot use medication which denies or forbids the illness to be treated.

What is the contingency formula of *society* if one can rashly say that society develops contingency formulas to describe itself? What concept does a society create about the insecurity that it generates itself? Naturally, there are many of these, and the typical trend has been a so-called "post"-trend. That one can no longer say about society that it "is" this and that, but on the contrary that it *"is not"* this or that. Thus, saying that the current society is not modern, but rather postmodern, is not industrial, but rather post-industrial, is not capitalist, but post-capitalist – all these semantic generalisations starting with a "post" are expressions of the ontological insecurity of current society. With another concept, which fulfils the same function, society is being called "a learning society". Also, this concept expresses the openly felt contingency that today may be as it is, but tomorrow may easily be different.

With this we have remained bystanders in the argument about whether it is this-or-that. We cannot satisfy the concept of a "learning society" with a "yes" or "no" answer, but we can explain where this concept comes from. This is not something that we like or don't like, but rather a symptom of social conditions, and we can take a position regarding the consequences.

But the specific functional systems of society must also develop contingency formulas, because on the one hand, all functional systems mould their specific surroundings, while on the other hand, they perceive the surroundings as unapproachable, that is, as contingencies, and therefore must develop contingency formulas, as expressed by Luhmann, that is, formulas that allow for the abundance of opportunities to be handled.

Maybe the best known contingency formula is the concept of God in the functional system of religion. On the face of it, the concept of "God" represents someone or something that knows everything and has created everything. In other words, the concept of "God" indicates that not everything is possible, but also that not everything is incidental; at the same time the concept of God indicates that the possibility to receive knowledge about these opportunities and limits is not available for ordinary people. "God" is therefore, according to Luhmann, not a resource of certainty, but a resource of uncertainty. The background for this is the fact that the religion system is a functionally differentiated system, the special function of which is the observation of meaning. Meaning is the starting point for media, for world observation and communication media. In other words, meaning is the distinction that separates concepts and the world. However, the function of religion is to make meaning observable, that is, to re-establish the distinction between concepts and world within the concept of God. God is therefore that instance, which can observe meaning as – with Husserl's expression – the unobservable world ho-

rizon. As is recorded in the Gospel according to St. John: "In the beginning was the Word, and the Word was with God and the Word
was God."

Another contingency formula delivers modern art, since modern
art not only helps to depict the world, but also to constantly define its
own possibilities. Twentieth century avant-garde does not deal with
the question of what the world is like, but how and why something
became art – if conditions could also have been different. In a society
influenced by self-produced insecurity, art becomes self-defining to
an extreme degree.

A third contingency formula delivers science. What do we know
for sure about today's scientific propositions? Not that this or that is
the fact, but – "that further research is necessary." What we know for
is that we will never get a final answer, but rather that insecurity continues to rule. We know that we don't know what we don't know. Every research report therefore ends with a requirement for further research. The contingency formula for science is therefore a dispassion-
ate concept, presented by Luhmann: "limitationality" – that after the
presentation of partial results, one must always indicate the limited
and temporary character of these concepts.

As to the *educational system,* the contingency formula is: *cultivation*
– in German: Bildung. "With the concept of cultivation, the educational system reacts to the loss of external (societal, role-based), bind-
ing points about what a human being is or should be." (p. 186). As
Luhmann adds ironically: "The word 'cultivation' presents the educational system's contingency formula with the use of a beautiful word
package. It flows easily off the tongue." (p. 187).

As a result of the society's contingency, the concept of cultivation
at the same time has changed its character. Ever more people doubt
whether the concept of cultivation can be transformed into a standard
of cultivation: that one must think in a certain way, must have read
this and that literature, etc. Most certainly the cultivation concept has
been constituted by the fact that "we" can be distinguished from
"them", although cultivation cannot be viewed from within, but must
seen from the outside. Yes, some adhere to standards – but does this
as an expression of modesty, that is, thereby to receive means for handling contingency. But others – and clearly ever more people – see
cultivation as a reflective concept. A person can be cultivated only if

he/she is able to put him/herself in the place of others, that is to imagine the cultivation of others. Cultivation is therefore not anymore the distinction between, but the reflective *observation* of the distinction between "we" and "them". "Therefore cultivation can be acquired only when it is considered what others mean by this." (p. 191). In this version, scholarship is not a standard concept, but a reflective concept. An individual is cultivated when he/she is capable of noticing what constitutes the difference between me and you, us and them.

Another consequence is that when teaching, the teachers stimulate students to handle their social contingency: Instead of being helped simply to learn "something" students are helped to "learn to learn". They may not, after all, limit themselves to assigned study materials, but should be capable of grasping more than is intended. They must, as Luhmann says, not only "learn knowledge", but "learn to handle non-knowledge" – for instance, by being able to make decisions. The concept of knowledge, used by the educational system, is not the same as used by the scientific system, where it is a form of knowledge, the possible untruth of which has been tested (p. 98). No, the knowledge transmitted in the educational system is a form of knowledge that creates possibilities for giving the future life process a new direction (p. 97). The direct extension of this is the mantra "lifelong learning". In other words, this project is not a project that we should preferably handle according to standards (whether we like it or not?), but which we must handle analytically. In a society that is characterised by self-generated uncertainty, it is not strange that lifelong learning becomes a prominent concept. "What will be found in the 20th century, regardless of whether the concept of cultivation is used or not, is the adaptation of the educational system's contingency formula as a reaction to the loss of a well-founded "normative" guarantee." (p. 194).

Luhmann names two phenomena that symbolise this adaptation process. One of these is lifelong learning, which according to Luhmann primarily means that students are supposed to learn all their lives and consequently must possess the ability to learn. This expresses the insecurity of the educational system on an individual basis. The second phenomenon, which symbolises the contingency of the educational system, is the growing insecurity of the educational system regarding itself. The only thing that is known in the educational system is that it is unsure about its own validity and must therefore constantly change. It seems that the more conservative the government, the more it feels the need to change the educational system.

But my recurrent theme is that the phenomenon of a "learning society" is too important for normative handling: some rejoice, some are angry. But there is no reason to rejoice over the fact that the society is becoming contingent, and there is as little reason to believe that contingency will disappear, although we express our dissatisfaction about it.

No, today's society is characterised – maybe more than anything else – by the opportunity for abundance, that is the insecurity generated by the society itself. We must handle this analytically, that is, try to understand the special role and challenges for the educational system in such a society. And when we have understood it – or at least come closer to understanding it – we can delve operationally, well aware, that there is always the need for further research.

Keeping this in mind, Luhmann's book is, despite its incompleteness and terminological indistinctiveness, a good starting point.

Conclusion

This, then, ends my book. Summarising it in reverse order, its basis is the special characteristics of the educational system in a society characterised by its contingency: Education to hypercomplexity. The basic function of this emerging educational system is to teach individuals to manage complexity. They must be reflectively cultivated, they must be prepared for lifelong learning by having learnt to learn, and they must possess knowledge beyond the limits of fixed, factual knowledge.

This leads into the necessity to redescribe knowledge. Knowledge in itself can be defined as condensed observations. Its function is to manage complexity, based on the principle that complexity can manage complexity. A knowledgeable person is a person with a high level of cognitive complexity. In the emerging hypercomplex society, knowledge isn't just a fixed ability but a dynamic ability. This implies that one must be able to apply knowledge to itself. Applying knowledge to itself, a number of knowledge categories can be developed. In addition to first order factual knowledge, there is second order or recursive knowledge, knowledge of knowledge, e.g. knowledge of how to use one's knowledge. Third order knowledge is reflective or hyper-recursive knowledge, i.e. knowledge of the conditions on which knowledge is based. Finally, fourth order knowledge is the total, dynamic and self-developing knowledge system: All that we can know in distinction to what we cannot know.

Based on these knowledge categories, a redescription of teaching and learning categories can be made. Teaching is not just the teaching of factual knowledge but it is also the teaching of how to acquire the other types of knowledge, i.e. teaching the student to become a learner. And learning isn't just the accumulation of knowledge but includes assimilative and accommodative learning processes as well. One learns how to learn. And one learns how to re-shape one's knowledge system. Thus, the student learns not only to be qualified, i.e. to know many things, but also to be competent, i.e. to know how to use his/her knowledge, and to be creative in the sense that he/she is able to reflect on the conditions for his/her knowledge and to change these conditions. Finally, the student knows that what he/she reflectively knows is part of a dynamic, hyper-recursive but also limited knowledge system: the totality of what can be known.

Finally, this leads to a redescription of society's educational system at its organisational and technological level. Education cannot anymore be limited in time to youth and in space to educational institutions. Education must also take place outside schools and after the end of the individual's "learning years". One answer is provided by life-long learning institutions, workplace-based learning etc. Another – technological – answer is found in the development of e-learning as an educational infrastructure, i.e. as a digital medium for teaching.

However, in order to analyse and discuss e-learning in a pedagogical context, the framework of a media pedagogy must be developed, including a theory of media education (teaching of media), media socialisation (teaching of students living in a mediatised society) and educational media (the use of media for teaching). In order to understand the potential functions and contributions of e-learning systems, they must be described according to the above-mentioned categories of knowledge, teaching and learning. E-learning systems must be designed so that they can support not only the acquisition of factual knowledge, but also of recursive and reflective knowledge, i.e. of competences and creativity. Only understood and designed in this way, can e-learning be used as one of many tools for changing the so-called knowledge society into a knowing society.

List of Orginal Communications

The present book is based on the following articles, all of which have been re-written for this publication.

"Society's Educational System – an introduction to Niklas Luhmann's pedagogical theory". In: *Seminar. International Journal,* Lillehammer, Vol. 1, no. 1, 2005. 18 pp.

"Knowledge Society and Educational Institutions – Towards a Sociological Theory of Knowledge". In: AGORA No 8, March 2006. *Teachers Matter 05,* OECD, pp. 43-75.

"E-Learning – A Knowledge Theoretical Approach". To appear in Peter Ludes (ed.): *Convergence – Fragmentation: Media Technology and the Information Society.* Changing Media, Changing Europe. Intellect, Bristol and Portland, in press.

Literature

Niels Åkerstrøm Andersen: *Diskursive analysestrategier. Foucault, Koselleck, Laclau, Luhmann.* [Discoursive strategies of analysis. Foucault, Koselleck, Laclau, Luhmann]. Nyt fra Samfundsvidenskaberne. Copenhagen 1999.

P. Ariès: *Barndommens historie.* [The history of Childhood]. Nyt Nordisk Forlag, Copenhagen 1982.

Dirk Baecker: *Kommunikation.* Reclam, Leipzig 2005.

Dirk Baecker: *Form und Formen der Kommunikation.* Suhrkamp Verlag, Frankfurt a. M. 2005.

Gregory Bateson: "The Logical Categories of Learning and Communication." In: Gregory Bateson: *Steps to an Ecology of Mind.* The University of Chicago Press, Chicago and London 2000 [1972].

Daniel Bell: *The Coming of Post-Industrial Society.* Basic Books, New York 1973.

Max H. Boisot: *Information Space. A Framework for Learning in Organizations, Institutions and Culture.* Routledge, London and New York 1995.

Max H. Boisot: *Knowledge Assets. Securing Competitive Advantage in the Information Economy.* Oxford University Press, Oxford 1998.

George Spencer Brown: *Laws of Form.* George Allen and Unwin, London 1971.

Manuel Castells: *The Rise of the Network Society.* Blackwell Publishers, Malden MA, and Oxford, UK, 1996.

Jean Clam: *Was heißt, sich an Differenz statt an Identität orientieren?* UVK, Konstanz 2002.

Jean Clam: *Kontingenz, Paradox, Nur-Vollzug.* UVK, Konstanz 2004.

Edward Craig: *Knowledge and the state of nature : an essay in conceptual synthesis.* Clarendon Press, Oxford 1990.

John Dewey: *Experience and Education.* Touchstone, Simon & Schuster, New York 1997 [1938].

Hubert L. Dreyfus: *On the Internet.* Routledge, London 2001.

Richard Florida: *The Rise of the Creative Class.* Basic Books, New York 2002.

Heinz von Foerster: *Observing Systems.* Intersystem Publications. Seaside, California 1984.

Yvonne Fritze, Geir Haugsbakk and Yngve Nordkvelle: "Tema: Mediepedagogikk" [Theme: Media Pedagogy], in *Norsk Medietidsskrift* årg. 11 nr. 3, 2004.

Martin Heidegger: *Sein und Zeit* [Being and Time]. Max Niemeyer, Tübingen 1986 [1927].

Stig Hjarvard: *Det selskabelige samfund* [The Social Society]. Forlaget Samfundslitteratur, Copenhagen 2005.

Detlef Horster: *Niklas Luhmann.* Verlag C. H. Beck, Munich 1997.

Edmund Husserl: *Fænomenologiens idé* [The Idea of Phenomenology]. Hans
Reitzels Forlag, Copenhagen 1997 [1907].

Edmund Husserl: *Cartesianische Meditationen* [Cartesian Meditations]. Felix
Meiner Verlag, Hamburg 1987 [1929].

Stuart Kauffman: *Investigations.* Oxford University Press, Oxford 2000.

Søren Harnow Klausen: *Reality Lost and Found. An Essay on the Real-
ism-Antirealism Controversy.* University Press of Southern Denmark,
Odense 2004.

Thomas S. Kuhn: *Die Struktur wissenschaftlicher Revolutionen.* Suhrkamp
Verlag, Frankfurt a. M. 1967.

Per Fibæk Laursen: *Den autentiske lærer* [The Authentic Teacher]. Gyldendal,
Copenhagen 2004.

Dieter Lenzen and Niklas Luhmann (eds.): *Bildung und Weiterbildung im
Erziehungssystem.* Suhrkamp Verlag, Frankfurt a. M. 1997.

Niklas Luhmann: *Soziologische Aufklärung 2. Aufsätze zur Theorie der
Gesellschaft.* Westdeutscher Verlag, Erlangen 1975.

Niklas Luhmann: *Liebe als Passion.* Suhrkamp Verlag, Frankfurt a. M. 1982.

Niklas Luhmann: *Soziale Systeme.* Suhrkamp Verlag, Frankfurt a. M. 1984.

Niklas Luhmann: *Die Wirtschaft der Gesellschaft.* Suhrkamp Verlag, Frankfurt
a. M. 1988.

Niklas Luhmann: *Die Wissenschaft der Gesellschaft.* Suhrkamp Verlag, Frankfurt a. M. 1990.

Niklas Luhmann: "Das Kind als Medium der Erziehung." In: *Zeitschrift für
Pädagogik,* no. 1, 1991.

Niklas Luhmann: *Das Recht der Gesellschaft.* Suhrkamp Verlag, Frankfurt a. M.
1993.

Niklas Luhmann: *Social Systems.* Stanford University Press, Stanford, California 1995 [first German version 1984].

Niklas Luhmann: *Die Kunst der Gesellschaft.* Suhrkamp Verlag, Frankfurt a. M.
1995.

Niklas Luhmann: *Soziologische Aufklärung 6. Die Soziologie und der Mensch.*
Westdeutscher Verlag, Erlangen 1995.

Niklas Luhmann: *Die Realität der Massenmedien. 2. erweiterte Auflage.*
Westdeutscher Verlag, Erlangen 1996.

Niklas Luhmann: *Die Gesellschaft der Gesellschaft.* Suhrkamp Verlag, Frankfurt
a. M. 1997.

Niklas Luhmann: *Art as a Social System.* Stanford University Press, Stanford
2000.

Niklas Luhmann: *Die Religion der Gesellschaft.* Suhrkamp Verlag, Frankfurt a.
M. 2000.

Niklas Luhmann: *Die Politik der Gesellschaft.* Suhrkamp Verlag, Frankfurt a. M.
2000.

Niklas Luhmann: *Das Erziehungssystem der Gesellschaft.* Suhrkamp Verlag, Frankfurt a. M. 2002.

Niklas Luhmann: "Erziehender Unterricht als Interaktionssystem" [1985]. In: Niklas Luhmann: *Schriften zur Pädagogik.* Edited by Dieter Lenzen. Suhrkamp Verlag, Frankfurt a. M. 2004.

Niklas Luhmann: "Systeme verstehen Systeme" [1986]. In: Niklas Luhmann: *Schriften zur Pädagogik.* Edited by Dieter Lenzen. Suhrkamp Verlag, Frankfurt a. M. 2004.

Niklas Luhmann: "Sozialisation und Erziehung" [1987]. In: Niklas Luhmann: *Schriften zur Pädagogik.* Edited by Dieter Lenzen. Suhrkamp Verlag, Frankfurt a. M. 2004.

Niklas Luhmann: "Das Erziehungssystem und die Systeme seiner Umwelt" [1996]. In: Niklas Luhmann: *Schriften zur Pädagogik.* Edited by Dieter Lenzen. Suhrkamp Verlag, Frankfurt a. M. 2004.

Niklas Luhmann and Karl Eberhard Schorr (eds.): *Zwischen Technologie und Selbstreferenz.* Suhrkamp Verlag, Frankfurt a. M. 1982.

Niklas Luhmann and Karl Eberhard Schorr (eds.): *Zwischen Intransparenz und Verstehen.* Suhrkamp Verlag, Frankfurt a. M. 1986.

Niklas Luhmann and Karl Eberhard Schorr (eds.): *Zwischen Anfang und Ende.* Suhrkamp Verlag, Frankfurt a. M. 1990.

Niklas Luhmann and Karl Eberhard Schorr (eds.): *Zwischen Absicht und Person.* Suhrkamp Verlag, Frankfurt a. M. 1992.

Niklas Luhmann and Karl Eberhard Schorr (eds.): *Zwischen System und Umwelt.* Suhrkamp Verlag, Frankfurt a. M. 1996.

William Lyons: *Gilbert Ryle. An Introduction to his Philosophy* The Harvester Press, Sussex 1980.

Helle Mathiasen: *Personlige bærbare computere i undervisningen* [Personal Portable Computers in Education]. Danmarks Pædagogiske Universitet, Copenhagen 2002.

Maurice Merleau-Ponty: *Phénoménologie de la perception* [The Phenomenology of Perception]. Editions Gallimard, Paris 1945.

Ministry of Science, Technology and Innovation: *Perspektiver for kompetenceudvikling – rapport om e-læring* [Perspectives for Competence Development – report on e-learning]. Copenhagen 2003.

Yngve Nordkvelle: *Forelesningen som undervisningsvirksomhet* [The Lecture as Educational Activity]. Unpublished manus, High School of Lillehammer, no publication year.

Tor Nørretranders: *Stedet som ikke er. Fremtidens nærvær, netværk og Internet* [The Place which does not Exist. Future's Presence, Network and Internet]. Aschehaug, Copenhagen 1997.

OECD: *Knowledge Management in the Learning Society.* OECD, Paris 2000.

OECD: *Innovations in the Knowledge Economy.* OECD, Paris 2004.

OECD: *Teachers Matter. Attracting, Developing and Retaining Effective Teachers.* OECD, Paris 2005.

Alexander von Oettingen: *Undervisningens Paradoks* [The Paradox of Education]. Klim, Copenhagen 2002.

Seymour Papert: *Mindstorms: Children, Computers, and Powerful Ideas.* Basic Books, New York 1980.

Edith Penrose: *The Theory of the Growth of the Firm.* Oxford University Press, Oxford 1959.

Michael Polanyi: *Personal Knowledge.* University of Chicago Press, Chicago 1958.

Michael Polanyi: *The Tacit Dimension.* Peter Smith, Gloucester, MA 1983 [1966].

Lars Qvortrup: *Det hyperkomplekse samfund* [The hypercomplex society]. Gyldendal, Copenhagen 1998.

Lars Qvortrup: *Det lærende samfund* [The learning society]. Gyldendal, Copenhagen 2001.

Lars Qvortrup: "Cyberspace as Representation of Space Experience: In Defence of a Phenomenological Approach". In: Lars Qvortrup (ed.): *Virtual Space. Spatiality in Virtual Inhabited 3D Worlds.* Springer-Verlag, London, Berlin, Heidelberg 2002.

Lars Qvortrup: *The Hypercomplex Society.* Peter Lang, New York 2003.

Lars Qvortrup: *Det vidende samfund* [The knowing society]. Unge Pædagoger, Copenhagen 2004.

Jens Rasmussen: *Undervisning i det refleksivt moderne* [Teaching in the Reflective Modern Society]. Hans Reitzel, Copenhagen 2004.

Walter Reese-Schäfer: *Luhmann zur Einführung.* Junius Verlag, Hamburg 1992.

Gilbert Ryle: *The Concept of Mind.* Hutchinson, London 1949.

Donald Schön: *The Reflective Practitioner. How Professionals Think in Action.* Arena, Great Britain 1991 [first edition 1983].

Claus Otto Scharmer: "Self-transcending Knowledge: Organizing around Emerging Realities". In: Ikujuru Nonaka and David Teece (eds.): *Managing Industrial Knowledge. Creation, Transfer and Utilization.* Sage Publications, London et al. 2001.

Michel Serres: *The Troubadour of Knowledge.* The University of Michigan Press, Ann Arbor 1997 [1991].

Nico Stehr: "Grenzenlose Wissenswelten?" In: Gertraud Koch (ed.): *Internationalisierung von Wissen. Multidisziplinäre Beiträge zu neuen Praxen des Wissenstransfers.* Röhrig Universitätsverlag, St. Ingbert 2006.

René Thom: *Structural Stability and Morphogenesis. An Outline of a General Theory of Models.* W. A. Benjamin, Reading, Massachusetts 1975.

René Thom: *Mathematical Models of Morphogenesis.* Ellis Horwood Limited, Chichester 1983.

L. S. Vygotsky: *Thought and Language*. MIT Press and Wiley, Cambridge MA. 1962 [1934].

L. S. Vygotsky: *Mind in Society*. Harvard University Press, Cambridge MA. 1978.

Paul Watzlawick, J. H. Beavin and D. D. Jackson: *Pragmatics of Human Communication*. Faber and Faber, London 1968.

Joseph Weizenbaum: *Computer Power and Human Reason: From Judgment to Calculation*. Freeman, San Francisco 1976.

Dan Zahavi: *Husserls fænomenologi* [Husserl's Phenomenology]. Gyldendal, Copenhagen 1997.

Dan Zahavi: *Fænomenologi* [Phenomenology]. Roskilde Universitetsforlag, Frederiksberg 2003.